Canadian Railway Records

A Guide for Genealogists

Revised and Expanded

Althea Douglas, MA, CG(C)
&
J. Creighton Douglas, BSc

MULTI PATRIAE
PRIORES ✦ MULTAE

The Ontario Genealogical Society
Toronto, 2004

Further copies of this book and information about the Society can be obtained by writing to:

The Ontario Genealogical Society
Suite 102, 40 Orchard View Boulevard
Toronto ON M4R 1B9
Canada

Library and Archives Canada Cataloguing in Publication
Douglas, Althea, 1926–
   Canadian railway records : a guide for genealogists / Althea Douglas & J. Creighton Douglas. — Rev. and expanded.
Includes bibliographical references and index.
ISBN 0-7779-2142-1

   1. Railroads—Canada—Employees—Archival resources. 2. Railroad companies—Canada—Archival resources. 3. Canada—Genealogy—Archival resources. 4. Railroads—Canada—Bibliography.

I. Douglas, J. Creighton, 1924– II. Ontario Genealogical Society. III. Title.
CS83.D68 2004   929'.371   C2004-905913-0

Cover Photo: Engineer in cab. Admired and envied by small boys all along the tracks, the engineer who drove the great steam engines held the glamour job. This is Engineer L.L. Wood in the cab of engine 6154, Canadian National Railway. Photo by Nicholas Morant, National Film Board of Canada; Library and Archives Canada, PA-153050

Published by The Ontario Genealogical Society
Suite 102, 40 Orchard View Boulevard
Toronto ON M4R 1B9
Canada
416-489-0734
provoffice@ogs.on.ca
www.ogs.on.ca

Published with assistance from the Ontario Ministry of Culture

Contents

Acknowledgements

Our thanks to the many archivists, librarians and association volunteers who took time to answer our questions. To Library and Archives Canada, to RG 30/R231 archivist Michael Dufresne, genealogist Mary Munk, and the many other archivists whom we consulted, our deep appreciation for helping us find our way between the older records and inventories and new accessions being electronically processed.

We must all be grateful to the late Don Whiteside who, way back in 1992 started us looking into what railway records might exist and encouraged us to write a Guide for Genealogists. The OGS published it in 1994 and reprinted it a year later. Now we have a whole new group of OGS staff and volunteers who have helped with this new edition, in particular, Ruth Chernia whose advice and professional skills have added greatly to this new volume.

Althea Douglas, MA, CG(C) and J. Creighton Douglas BSC
2004

Introduction

This *Guide to Canadian Railway Records* was written for genealogists and family historians and first published in 1994. A decade later it is time for an update; exciting new sources have been discovered and explored, new documents have been located and others have been released by Government departments and boards to the National Archives that, in turn, have become part of Library and Archives Canada. Moreover, since 1994, the Internet has become an important resource for researchers, so this edition offers guidelines to useful sources and URLs.

There is no way this edition can list every library, museum and archive across the country and the personnel-related railway-generated documents they contain. Nor is there space to describe the hundreds of companies that actually ran trains in what is now Canada. However, there are books that do, and Internet databases to help track down records.

This Guide will tell you how to find the lists of companies; the addresses of libraries, museums, archives and historical societies; and what sorts of records you may find as you hunt. The discoveries are yours to make.

This Guide is not written for the railway hobbyists, professionals or historians who have produced countless books detailing the history of Canadian railways and the equipment they used. Nevertheless, to work effectively in railway records, you must become familiar with some of this history. We will try to point you in the right directions to do such homework—but only you can do it.

While the bulk of surviving railway records consists of the documents that define corporate entities and legal connections, this book will focus on material that tells about individual people. Where there are no names, records are not much use to genealogists. In huge payrolls where there are hundreds of names, what you can find may only confirm what you have to know to find your railwayman.

Records of the many subsidiary companies that operated the railway-owned hotels, steamships, telegraph services, grain elevators, produce terminals and land development schemes are not included, although we try to point the way to them. The one type of non-company documents that we have actively sought are employees' association and union records that name individual employees.

Biographical information, if published in trade or union magazines, books or newspapers, is open to researchers. Most records, however, are subject to a minimum thirty-year cut-off date. That takes us back to the mid-1970s depending on when you are reading this.

Railway transportation in Canada began in 1836. The summer of 1960 saw the end of the era of steam throughout the country. So we are looking at over a century of steam locomotion, a decade of transition to diesel (1949–1959) and some fifteen years plus of diesel operation. For that reason, most explanations here relate to steam operations, and a way of life unfamiliar to many researchers. Some railwaymen moved as often as clergymen or bank clerks. Others found a place they liked, a comfortable run and used their increasing seniority to stay put. Chapter Two will explain some of the facts of railway life in the long era of steam.

Do not let your thinking be limited by borders. Our vast rail transportation system was built with few considerations for national boundaries, much less those of the provinces. Canadian lines crossed back and forth into the United States and many American lines served Canadian towns and cities. Divisions often ignore provincial borders.

There are thousands of books about railways and they range from small and inexpensively printed pamphlets that preserve a retired conductor's reminiscences and anecdotes, to glossy picture books that illustrate locomotives, coaches or the architecture of stations or roundhouses. Whatever aspect of railway operations you want to know about, rest assured that someone has written about it, and almost always found pictures to illustrate it.

We have provided a brief bibliography, trying to note the books that, in themselves, have good bibliographies or notes. As well, some of the various trade and company magazines are included, but you may well find others in the collection of some local institution.

Since the technologies of steam locomotion and photography may be said to have grown up together, the pictorial record is vast. Railway enthusiasts love to take pictures and always have, so family historians have a good chance of finding pictures of station agent great-grandfather's station or fireman grandfather's engine, often with the ancestor posed in front. Since railway enthusiasts take naturally to technology, they have also found their place on the Internet, where Web sites deal with almost every aspect of railroading. Also on the Internet are library catalogues of books and archival catalogues of documents, all of which can be searched at home. Again, this guide can only try to suggest some possible ways to search, but cannot cover every source.

After the first edition came out we were asked a great many questions on how to find information about train wrecks or accidents. Some documents have been released to Library and Archives Canada, some published information has been located and there is a new chapter covering the subject. As well, when searching for nineteenth-century knitting-machine patents I came across hundreds of "improvements" to railway equipment. I am hoping that a chapter on to how to find such patents will save our readers some of the frustrations I experienced.

This book has been a joint effort but we each have our own areas of expertise. Creighton wrote much of the material on the railway way of life, working conditions and so on. Althea did the archival work checking documents and bibliographical data and wrote about libraries and archives so, inevitably, on occasion we wrote in the first person singular and at other times in the first person plural.

The records of Canadian railways offer such a variety of information and experience that there is some aspect that will intrigue almost everyone. So we add a consumer warning: railways are highly addictive and can absorb all your free time and available money.

Althea and Creighton Douglas
Ottawa, 2004

Women oiling locomotive

Railways were a man's world — *except* during wartime when women replaced men in many jobs. Here two women give up cleaning house to clean a fast freight engine in a roundhouse during World War II.

One

Getting Started

Three Facts to Know

Before plunging into railway records you must know three things about U.R. Ancestor (let's shorten that to "U.R.," which his friends pronounced "You're"):

1. What railway(s) employed U.R.?
2. In what Region, what Division, Station or Section did he work?
3. What was his trade or job?

It will help answer these questions if you can find out two more facts:

4. Where did the family live when U.R. was with the railway?
5. Where did he retire and when?

Sorry about the sexist "he." Women did work in railway offices, and a Station Agent's wife might do many paid and unpaid chores, but it was essentially *a man's world*. Except in wartime, if a woman worked for the railway she sat at a typewriter, switchboard, occasionally a telegraph key or perhaps was a nurse assisting the Medical Officer. Moreover, it was the sisters or daughters of railway employees who were likely to get such jobs. Until well past the middle of the twentieth century, again with wartime exceptions, women were expected to leave a job when they married. A "respectable" unmarried woman could not travel unchaperoned in the company of men, thus secretaries were usually men who could travel with executives in a business car. Dr. O.M. Solandt, broke with this tradition "...and chose a woman who had been with the CN for many years and trained many of the male secretaries." As he explained, "I would not be travelling as much as other vice-presidents, and if I travelled in a business car I would take my wife along as well as Mary"(MacKay, 1992, pp. 201–2). Clerk and Chief Clerk were posts of considerable responsibility and also normally held by men (see Glossary, Appendix A).

You Must Know the Railway

This is one fact you must determine at the outset of your quest. Loyalty to THE Railway that employed U.R., his relatives and friends, is often a firmly rooted family tradition. If so, your only problem is one of historical research into its various incarnations.

While most railway employees remained with the same line throughout their career, the name of the company might change more than once during that time. My U.R., born in Moncton, New Brunswick, in 1886, started as an apprentice to his father with the ICR (Intercolonial Railway) in 1900, rose in the ranks of the expanding CGR (Canadian Government Railways), was moved to Toronto in the 1930s by the CNR (Canadian National Railway) and retired from the CNR on an ICR Pension in Montreal in 1951.

Start with the Family

When *all* you know is that "U.R. Ancestor worked for the Railway," the first step (as any genealogist knows) is to question family members and friends who may know something. Ask where the family lived. Was it a CPR or CNR town? Or served by some other line? Ask what U.R.'s job was. Even if they only know "U.R. was away a lot but I don't know what he did," then you can be pretty sure that he was not a shop, office or station employee. Look for him in the running trades, maintenance of way, engineering or construction (of bridges, stations etc.). Some higher level executives also travelled extensively.

Look for Passes

Railway workers and their families were entitled to passes. These ranged from "work passes" for free travel on railway business to levels of non-business travel for the worker and his family based on seniority. Officials often held passes from other lines allowing them to travel on most of the railways across North America. It was also possible for families to travel free over other lines, usually on a one-trip basis. Long-service employees often received a "gold pass" when they retired. These often turn up in scrapbooks or collections of railway ephemera. Did someone in the family keep a pass, perhaps in some scrapbook as a souvenir of a holiday trip? That will tell you what railway employed U.R. and what his job was, even if it was issued for travel on another railway system.

Retirement at Sixty-five?

Retirement is another place to start. Most railway companies developed pension plans or benevolent funds at an early date. Benevolent plans assisted workers injured in accidents (many were), or paid something to the widows, or allowed retirement before age sixty-five in cases of failing health. Plans varied and when one company absorbed another, plans might be kept separate and survive when the original company was long gone. The Provident Fund of the ICR & PEI Railway was paying pensions for decades after it became part of the CNR.

Not until the end of World War II can you count on retirement at age sixty-five. At the turn of the century retirement was a matter of personal choice, state of health, and the boss's views of an older employee's value to the company. In the 1920s when sixty-five was becoming accepted as the age of retirement, the ICR & PEI Provident Fund Board records that "we have several men on our pay list at the present time who have passed the 70 year mark," who apparently "wish to continue at work" and so their cases have never come before the Board (Minutes, 1923–6, p. 217). The 1930s depression may have shifted attitudes, but wartime staffing shortages again meant delayed retirement.

Nevertheless, if you know when someone was born, sixty-five years later look for a story about that retirement. In a railway town like Moncton or Stratford, the local newspaper almost certainly covered it. U.R. might rank quite low in the pecking order, but long service did count for something; there might be a presentation by an official of some importance whose presence justified a reporter's time. Also check company, trade association and union magazines and newsletters. Retirement stories may tell where and when a person joined the company, whether they held union posts, or give other career details.

One source of career and retirement notices for anyone in any sort of supervisory position is *The Railway and Shipping World* (available on microfiche), which started publication in Toronto March 1898 (Angus, 1998, pp. 47–56). In 1906 it became *The Railway and Marine World*, in 1912, *Canadian Railway and Marine World*, then, in January 1937, *Canadian Transportation.*

A Thousand Canadian Railways!

Assuming you know the railway U.R. retired from, read up on its corporate history. Find out which lines merged to form it, or which lines it took under its wing. Remember there was no CNR before 1919, just smaller money-losing systems. For an idea of the orders of magnitude we are dealing with, compare the three-page list of some 134 railways whose records survive in England, Scotland and Wales (Richards, 1989) with Noel G. Butlin's *Finding List of Canadian Railway Companies Before 1916* that lists over 1,080 companies.

Lines of Country

For anyone with an interest in these companies, a really great reference atlas was published in 1997. Geoffrey Matthews brought his cartographic skills to a book by Christopher Andreae that is helpful in both locating and tracking railroad ancestors, and indeed, any migrants. *Lines of Country: An Atlas of Railway and Waterway History in Canada* will show you where, and *when*, every rail line and waterway in Canada was built, operated and abandoned. Mind you, it's not simple to read: the maps are detailed, the text absolutely packed with information, the illustrations fascinating, and there is a bibliography and index. Near the end is a "Synoptic History of Railway Companies" that lists which lines were absorbed by which major company.

Another good source, if you can follow the brief and somewhat cryptic entries, is the revised edition of Robert Dorman and D.E. Stoltz *A Statutory History of the Steam and Electric Railways of Canada 1836–1986* (1987).

Once you know the name of the railway, you will find brief but readable accounts of many small lines in an early edition of *The Encyclopedia of Canada* [hereafter *EC* '40]. Edited by a noted historian just before World War II, this is an invaluable guide to the recent past. Most libraries will have a copy, although probably now in the stacks. In the 1930s railway service mattered and these volumes usually state, in the city or town entries, which railways served which towns and cities. For example, in Vol. V, p. 245 we learn that Richmond, Quebec, was on the CNR; Richmond, Ontario, on the CPR; and Ridgetown, Ontario, on the Michigan Central and Père Marquette Railways.

If you suspect a local railway became part of the CNR, you can make a quick check of the Index of the old (1968) *Union Catalogue of Manuscripts in Canadian Repositories* for the railway company's name. If any records survive, there will be an entry in the index indicating they are now "with CNR records." This does not work as well for the CPR, which was also a large fish that swallowed many smaller lines. In most cases, however, the CPR leased these companies and each corporate entity remained separate and kept its own name.

How Is It Indexed?

The shifts in railway company names can be a trap. Surviving records, in particular those in local libraries, museums and small archives may be indexed under the name of the company that appears on the document. Whether or not the originating railway company, or the present name of the company appears in an index may depend on how much the indexer knew about railway history. Not all indexes are as complete as the one in the Toronto Public Library's North York Central Library Canadiana Collection that gives the main company name, then picks up every obscure, small, local line mentioned in the documents. This index is a valuable source of information on southern Ontario companies.

On the Internet—New Databases

In October 2002 the National Library and National Archives of Canada merged to become Library and Archives Canada (LAC). By the spring of 2004 a new joint Web site was in place: <www.collectionscanada.ca> replaces the addresses of the two former sites <www.archives.ca> and <www.nlc-bnc.ca>. Links and bookmarks pointing to the old addresses are automatically forwarded, and probably will be for some time, but you should update yours to reflect the changes to the site.

Both the Union Catalogue of Canadian Libraries' published material, AMICUS, and the Archives' computerized inventory, ArchiviaNet, can be searched at this site. For the union catalogue of Canadian archival holdings (a separate site) see *Archives Canada* below.

While at the LAC Web site, look for a section, "Canada, By Train," intended for a general audience but with a surprising amount of railway lore in readily accessible format, with photographs, illustrations, sound and video. There is an "Index of Railway Companies" (with links for about 38 companies, mentioned in the text) and a searchable database of the Library's Merrilees Transportation Collection.

On 20 October 2001 the Canadian Council of Archives launched the *Canadian Archival Information Network* (CAIN) that provided access to descriptions of most of the holdings of archival institutions across Canada. On 17 October 2003 CAIN in turn became Archives Canada <www.archivescanada.ca>. This cross-country service should not be confused with Library and Archives Canada in Ottawa (whose new URL is <www.collectionscanada.ca>) and which supports Archives Canada but is quite a different institution. Think of them as cousins with similar names — a problem most genealogists are familiar with.

Archives Canada is a trans-Canada operation. Archival institutions all across the country, holding physical documents such as texts, maps, artwork and more, have been asked to produce standardized detailed descriptions of their holdings, with regular updates on new accessions. These are then made available through this national Internet database. By its nature, this is a work in progress; persevere and it should turn up the same sort of information the printed *Union List of Manuscripts in Canadian Repositories* once offered us, but in greater detail. It will certainly be of assistance in locating records of all sorts. However, the more specific you can make your search terms the fewer "finds" you will have to sort through. Use the "Advanced Search" screen to include several limiting search terms.

Somewhere in the 500 plus issues of *Canadian Rail*, published since 1949 by the Canadian Railway Historical Association, there will almost certainly be an article giving detailed facts about any rail line you seek, be it one of the smallest, the Asbestos and Danville Railway (issue No. 414,

Jan.–Feb. 1990), or the component companies acquired by the CPR (No.400, Sept.–Oct. 1987). A searchable index to the bimonthly *Canadian Rail* is now available on the association's Web site <www.exporail. org/association/intro_crha.htm>.

The Internet offers a great many Web sites devoted to railway history, lines or companies; and railway equipment and former stations, with links to more of the same. However, as with *Canadian Rail* articles, what you can find on the Internet will depend on whether some individual has contributed knowledge to some Web site, and how extensive that knowledge is. You can start with the CRHS Web site (above) or Google for individual lines. You will probably bring up a very mixed bag, waste a lot of time, but perhaps be lucky.

- <www.railways.incanada.net/> will bring up Colin Churcher's Railway Pages. His interest is primarily in the history of railways of Eastern Ontario, which is hardly "Canada." Here, as on most Web sites, the links have a local focus.

- <www.bytownrailwaysociety.ca/> welcomes you to the Bytown Railway Society, whose members volunteer with restoration of equipment at the Canadian Museum of Science and Technology in Ottawa. Like so many CRHS members, it is primarily the equipment they care about.

- <www.proto87.org/ca/> is devoted to the history of a single company, the Canada Atlantic Railway, built by lumber baron, J.R. Booth, in eastern Ontario from Georgian Bay down into Vermont in the USA.

- <www.ovar.ca/> is the Ottawa Valley Associated Railroaders, whose interest is in model trains—not former railroad employees.

Railway Guides and Timetables

A less obvious source of information is the *Official Railway Guides*. These are compilations of timetables put together for shippers and, like telephone books and directories, these are ephemera, out of date within six months or a year, but often taken home and kept by employees. They can turn up in libraries, railway museums or other collections under a variety of titles and put together by different publishing companies. The most complete Canadian collection is at the University of Guelph (see Works Consulted). When rail transportation was dominant, some appeared monthly. They are usually arranged by company and indexed by place (destination).

What was the Kick and Push?

For the uninitiated, it is bad enough that most railways are called by their initials—CNR, CPR, GTR (see Appendix B); but what if you are told "U.R. started with the Kick and Push" or the "Dust and Rust" or the "Push, Pull and Jerk." There are similar joking names for large and small lines from Bonavista to Vancouver Island, but how is anyone who is not a Railway buff expected to know them?

How do you find out? Presumably the Kick and Push was some line named the K_____ & P_____. Was there one called Kennebecasis & Penobsquis? Kamloops & Penticton? Did U.R. come from New Brunswick? British Columbia? No, he was from Ontario. Hmmm? Kitchener? No, that was Berlin pre-1914. Kingston and Prescott? Peterborough? P-what?

In addition to Dorman and Stoltz and *The Encyclopedia of Canada*, other books in the Bibliography have indexes or lists of railways. Check two or three and you will find there was a Kingston and Pembroke Railway. On the Internet, using Google to search for "Kick and Push," and limiting it to Canadian references, this nickname was confirmed on half a dozen regional tourist promotion pages. So, if U.R.'s family originated in eastern Ontario, this is your line because it did become part of the CPR. So did the "Push, Pull and Jerk"—that's the Pontiac & Pacific Junction Railway, and the Dominion Atlantic Railway (Dust and Rust) down in Nova Scotia (leased by the CPR in 1914). "Get There Perhaps" was the Grand Trunk Pacific, "Never Start on Time" the Niagara, St. Catharines and Toronto. If you browse through back issues of *Canadian Rail* you will learn of many others, but alas, there is no easy guide through this alphabet soup.

Company Towns

If you do not know which railway, but do know the community where the family lived you might have the answer to the question; some places were served by one line only. That will be The Railway that people in the town worked for. Stratford, Ontario, a divisional point on the CNR (formerly Grand Trunk) was the site of large locomotive repair shops (*EC '40, VI, 73*). Stratford had no CPR service.

Most large towns had two or more railways, but one usually was dominant, as in Smiths Falls, Ontario, which was "a divisional point of the Canadian Pacific Railway, employing 1,000 men" (*EC '40, VI, 37*), but only a minor stop on a line the CNR used mostly for freight. Similarly, Moncton, New Brunswick, was a CNR (ICR) town with the headquarters for the Atlantic Region and large car and locomotive shops. A CN branch line linked Moncton to Saint John so technically that city was on both the CNR and CPR, but at Saint John the CPR main line ended at the ferry terminal (to Digby, Nova Scotia), CPR transatlantic ships docked at Saint John when Quebec City was icebound; many CPR people lived there, so it was essentially a CPR town. Timetables, often consolidated for the convenience of shippers in variously titled official railway guides, will show what trains actually ran to a place, and how often. This should give some idea of which line was the important one in any community.

A junction point like St. Johns (now St-Jean sur Richelieu), Quebec, which was served by the Canadian National; Canadian Pacific; Central Vermont; Quebec, Montreal and Southern; Delaware and Hudson; and Rutland Railways (*EC '40, V, 324*) does present a problem, as do terminal cities like Halifax, Montreal, Toronto, Winnipeg and Vancouver. However, almost all big cities have runs of annual city directories. Where you have a choice of companies, try checking these directories; individual listings often include the company a resident worked for. Check for all family members, remembering that nepotism was a railway tradition.

As well, it will be a matter of local lore which railway served a town. If *Lines of Country* or *The Encyclopedia of Canada* fail you, skim through a local or regional history (there are special bibliographies listing these) and ask the local library, museum and historical society what records they have of local railways. Librarians and curators ought to know what has been written about a region's railways, if only because the authors pestered them for pictures and records. Some may hold collections of business papers, memorabilia and ephemera used to mount special displays.

Ask particularly about any railway historical group in the area that might be able to help you determine what Division, Station, or even what Section you ought to focus on. If you are not sure of these terms, read Chapter Two or check the Glossary.

Do Your Homework

Once you have discovered what companies U.R. Ancestor worked for over the years, the next step is to find what has been written about those railways, and perhaps about your family. Because photography is a technology that came along not much later than steam locomotion, the photographic records of railway history are extensive and almost every book on every branch line has photographs. Who knows, there might even be photographs of U.R.

If U.R. did indeed start with the Kick and Push, you are in luck because Carol Bennett has written a delightful history, *In Search of the K & P*, with interviews, reminiscences, pictures and names.

Books and Bibliographies

How does one find out about books like this? The proper way is to consult bibliographies; there are three listed in the Bibliography to this book that, if you can lay your hands on them, will take you up to 1980 (in addition a recent work relates primarily to British Columbia Railways). After 1980 you must use library catalogues. Fortunately, many can be searched on the Internet, including the Library and Archives of Canada's AMICUS, which is a union catalogue of almost all libraries across Canada.

While catalogue entries tell you what books exist, they do not tell you if the books contain information useful for your purpose. I found Carol Bennett's book when browsing in the Railway section in the Ottawa Public Library. Second-hand bookstores are also fun. An Ottawa Antiquarian Book Fair turned up *Clark's History of the Early Railways in Nova Scotia*. It had no publication date, but included "Seniority Lists" from 1925 for Engineers, Firemen, Conductors and Trainmen with the W.& A.R. [Windsor & Annapolis, which became part of the "Dust and Rust," which the CPR absorbed]. "Very scarce, priced at $60.00," said the book dealer. I did not buy it, knowing the National Library would have a copy. I did buy the 1974 *Credit Valley Railway … A History* by James Filby for $8.00.

Browsing may work in cities where second-hand book dealers gather, but for many people, although Internet dealers can find out-of-print books for you, looking through them is not an option. Moreover, browsing is not systematic research. For books and theses published after 1980, look through the subject indexes of both current and older editions of *Books in Print* and *Canadian Books in Print* (most public libraries, and many bookstores have copies). Even small reference libraries usually have runs of the *Canadian Periodical Index*, while the National Library's series *Canadian Theses* is a guide to their program for preserving theses in microform, available by interlibrary loan.

If you have a computer and an Internet connection you can search AMICUS, the Union Catalogue of Canadian Library resources, as well as many larger libraries' catalogues. Because library cataloguers frequently use Library of Congress subject headings, you should try a subject search under both Railway (Canadian and British usage) and Railroad (American usage). Any Canadian reference library ought to have the company histories and major works listed in the Bibliography. Small branch libraries tend to stock the recent "picture books" devoted to locomotives, stations and the like. For the Kick and Push lines and their ilk, you might start by contacting a library in the region where your interest lies.

Also check with local historical societies and museums, especially railway museums and restored stations (which often house local museums). These may help by directing you to any railway historical group in the area, or even introducing you to individual old-timers. In *The Guide to Canada's Railway Heritage Museums and Attractions*, Lawrence Adams lists all railway museums across Canada, giving full information and a map to simplify finding them, as well as providing a three-page "List of Designated Railway Stations, June 1992," and an address list of many railway interest groups, some of which are branches of the Canadian Railroad Historical Association. An updated second edition, compiled by Daryl T. Adair and published in 2001, should offer reasonably current information.

You can locate most libraries and other record repositories through the Internet. However library reference sections will have (or be able to access) current versions of the *Directory of Libraries in Canada*, the *Official Directory of Canadian Museums and Related Institutions* and perhaps the *Directory of Canadian Archives* and the *Directory of Historical Organizations in the United States and Canada*. Since the entries overlap in many cases, addresses and collection information should be easy to check. However, printed directories can be several years old, so it is wise to confirm addresses in current telephone directories or the Internet.

Hierarchy and Geography

The Hierarchy

Having determined what railway employed U.R. Ancestor, then learned when it began, where it ran, what company absorbed it—or what companies it absorbed, the next step is to figure out where U.R. belonged in the company hierarchy. The following is a simple outline of levels of management and the records they generated.

Head Office

The company head office is where the V.I.P.s make policy decisions; therefore many of the documents that originate there will survive in company archives. Few are of genealogical interest unless your ancestor was among the top executives, or corresponded with one of them. The CNR head office is in Montreal, but in 2001 when the CPR was split into five different companies, the railway head office moved to Calgary.

At headquarters are the offices of the President, assorted Vice Presidents in charge of this or that, and a number of Chiefs of various operations and departments. Office staffing would be similar to any head office of any large corporation of the era. Look for organization structure and names of senior executives in annual reports. This information is also found at least in part in the large system timetables. The many editions of *Who's Who in Railroading* (before 1930 *The Biographical Directory of Railway Officials of America*) list most officials of both American and Canadian railways down to the level of Division Superintendent, with a brief career outline.

Operations

Most companies separated train operations into Passenger Traffic and Freight Traffic. Railway equipment, its construction, repair and maintenance was divided between Motive Power (all locomotives) and Car Equipment (all railway cars, both freight and passenger). For most of the last century, the larger railway systems were divided and run on the basis of geographic regions.

Where it is possible to pinpoint the years U.R. Ancestor worked for a specific company, the annual reports for those years may provide a fuller understanding of the company's organizational structure at the time. Timetables can be useful; try to find an *Official Railway Guide*, which will consolidate many timetables for the use of shippers. These give the names of freight agents, station agents, passenger agents and others whom people doing business with railways on a regular basis would need to know.

Regional Headquarters

For any transcontinental line, expect to find at least an Eastern and Western region, as with the CPR, though smaller lines may have smaller regions. The CNR at one time had five regions: Atlantic, with Regional Headquarters at Moncton, St. Lawrence (Montreal), Great Lakes or Central (Toronto), Prairie (Winnipeg) and Western (Edmonton). The CPR had Eastern Lines and Western Lines, and within these, Districts. For example, the Quebec District extended from Quebec City to Brockville, Smiths Falls, Eganville, up to Chalk River and down to Wells River in Vermont, and included the Laurentian, Farnham, and Smiths Falls Divisions, plus the Ottawa, Montreal and Quebec Terminals.

Regional Headquarters were concerned with the overall management of everything within the Region (Divisions, shops, stations and termi-nals, etc.). Here you will find officials of General Superintendent level, and staffing similar to any branch office. Company archives will usually preserve the documentation of major decisions and activities within the Region or District. The big company shops, where locomotives and rolling stock were built and repaired, were major factors in the local economy. The shops employed a wide spectrum of skilled tradesmen, and functioned like any branch manufacturing organization. Within a Region or District, the day-to-day operations were handled by Divisions.

What Is a Division and Why Does It Matter?

A Division was essentially the distance that a nineteenth century steam locomotive could comfortably run without significant maintenance and in a working day (Barr, 1984, pp. 76–81). What with stops for water, coal and meeting other trains, this was about 120 to 150 miles. At each end would be a marshalling yard, a roundhouse and a maintenance facility. Freight engines were normally assigned to specific divisional points and changed off there, so ran back and forth between more or less the same places. Originally, passenger locomotives were changed off too, but later improvements to equipment allowed them to "run through." When diesel engines were introduced in the 1950s the old divisional points became redundant and many employees moved.

Division Headquarters were usually at the end away from the main terminal (for example, Smiths Falls, Ontario, not Montreal), and here you find the offices of the Division Superintendent and his Chief Clerk (*he who must be obeyed*), his Chief Engineer, Master Mechanic, Car Foreman, Roadmaster, Bridge and Building Superintendent, Chief Dispatcher, Division Passenger Agent and Division Freight Agent etc. Except for some milk runs, crews almost always lived at the divisional point. Here too will be found the whole range of employees who serviced the trains and locomotives, maintained tracks and rights of way, as well as the Division's executive level of operations. Local union lodges were also located at divisional points on a line.

The majority of railway employees related to and were paid in the Division they worked in, and in the running trades and maintenance of way, except for the "boomers," they seldom changed Division. Part of the craft's *mystery* was knowing every inch of track and what it *sounded* like as the train ran over it. Divisional records are broken down by trade or job groups. The running trades either made the engines go (engineers, firemen) or dealt with what the cars carried (conductors and brakemen, passenger or freight). Station staff and yard crews turn up together in some payrolls, occasionally with the section crews working out of the Station.

Lines of track were divided into "Sections." A Section was a specific short stretch of track designated by the Maintenance-of-Way Department to be regularly inspected and maintained by a Section foreman with a variable number of trackmen or sectionmen. These men will be found in Division or Station staff records and usually on Section payrolls, if such survive. On the other hand, the large gangs of labourers required for major track repairs, ballasting and even snow clearing in Terminals were usually recruited from the local labour pool and paid by the hour. Sometimes they turn up on payroll lists. However, unless you know the Division and better yet the Section, you will find yourself looking for the proverbial needle in a haystack.

What Else and Where?

Census Records

You know where U.R.'s family lived, and what railway he was employed with, but are not certain of his job. Have you looked in the census records? These usually give the occupation of the head of household, sometimes quite detailed. For example, in 1891, in North Bay, a city then served by the Canadian Pacific and Grand Trunk Railways, we find Patrick J. Gorman is "Asst. mechanical foreman railway shop," and other employments range from boiler maker through dining car conductor, railway car builder, steam railway assistant superintendent to telegraph messenger boy. There are 64 "Steam railway brakemen," 30 conductors, 29 engineers and 29 firemen, which suggests it was a divisional point on at least one line. A number of the young, unmarried steam railway brakemen lived at the local hotels.

This information was compiled by Gerald J. Neville, who, when he made an "Alphabetical Listing of Households" in the *1891 Census of North Bay* (1994) also tabulated an "Index of Railway Occupations." Not only is this a valuable tool for genealogists researching North Bay families, but for any railway researcher it shows which age groups were in what jobs. To know who was living in hotels or boarding houses, sheds light on how such a railway society worked. It is also easy to locate the family job links, like the Dreaney family, where Henry (age 28) and Thomas J. (age 26) are steam railway conductors, while James (age 23) is a steam railway brakeman, and William J (age 18) a steam railway car checker.

Nepotism, or All in the Family

It was not uncommon to find several members of a family employed by the same railway company, often over two or three generations. Nepotism was not the sin it is today. Indeed entrance into many long established Brotherhoods and Craft Guilds depended on there being a relative who was a member and would take the young man as his apprentice. Boys from railway families might start as "call boys" or newspaper vendors or "candy butchers" on passenger trains, learning what various jobs entailed. Where staff lists survive, knowing your ancestor's age or place of residence may be the one way to distinguish him from his uncle or cousin with the same name.

When Charles M. Hays joined GTR as General Manager on 1 January 1896, he tried to change things. A letter book, with copies of his correspondence, 30 September 1897–24 March 1899 is at Library and Archives Canada in RG 30 [Vol.1781]. By October 1897 Hays appears to have been going through payrolls and other financial records with a fine-tooth comb. On p. 4 is a Memo to Heads of Departments re relatives on the payrolls. "… the rules prohibiting the employment of sons or relations in the same department will hereafter be strictly enforced …"

However, when Hays came to the Grand Trunk from the Wabash Railroad, he brought F.H. McGuigan from the Wabash (15 February 1896) as General Superintendent of the GTR, and they then lured other Wabash men to the GTR. Not family, to be sure, but people they knew and had worked with on another railway.

Hays' letter-books reveal his grasp of detail, and his insistence on the need to get staffing, accounting and reporting uniform and standardized across the system. Hays turned the Grand Trunk from a company run poorly by absentee owners into one run efficiently in Canada. Alas, he drowned when the *Titanic* sank in 1912.

Radio Broadcasting for Trains

If someone told you that "U.R. went into broadcasting, but he got his start with the Railway" would it surprise you? It really happened. A curious bit of railway history is the CNR's radio broadcasting network, developed in the mid-1920s as "new entertainment" for train passengers.

Radio sets were placed in parlour cars or observation cars and carried programs broadcast from CNRM in Montreal and CNRO in Ottawa. These stations were soon joined by "The Voice of the Maritimes," CNRA, which broadcast from the CNR Offices in Moncton with a power of 500 watts and using a broadcasting tower set in the front lawn of the Atlantic headquarters building. In other centres, air time was bought from local stations (McNeil and Wolfe, 1982, pp. 177–93).

Except for CNRA [Atlantic?], the call letters were CNR plus the initial of the city. CNRW in Winnipeg, CNRS in Saskatoon, CNRE in Edmonton and CNRC in Calgary, served the prairies, with CNRV in Vancouver and CNRT in Toronto. Some programming was local and in addition to the staff announcers and technicians employed by the CNR, you might find a talented ancestor in their program listing in the newspapers. The CNR network was taken over by the Canadian Radio Broadcasting Commission (CRBC) which, when the Government changed in 1936, became the CBC. Some records of the CNR Radio Department are at LAC, in RG 30, and have been microfilmed, see Chapter Four.

Published Staff Lists

If U.R. started with the ICR between 1876 and 1925, or was employed by one of the smaller Government-owned systems, you have another source for staff lists: *Sessional Papers of the Dominion of Canada* (1868–1925). The 1878 papers include: "Statement showing names [and ages], occupation and salary of all persons except ordinary mechanics and labourers who were in the service of the Intercolonial Railway on 31 March, 1876 (Vol.11, vol.10, No.21).

Similar lists turn up annually, though their placement varies. By the beginning of the twentieth century even the "ordinary mechanics and labourers" in the Moncton shops are listed, though the ages are no longer given. These annual reports on the Government-operated railways continue to give a remarkable amount of staff information well into the 1920s. This source is discussed in detail in Chapter Four, p. 66. In Western Canada, early directories, both city and regional, sometimes include almost complete listings of CPR employees, see Chapter Five, p. 83.

In February 1943 a Canadian National Railway brakeman holds onto a boxcar. His job was one of the coldest of them all during the winter, one of the hottest in summer, and, in the early years before the advent of air brakes, among the most dangerous.

Two

The RR Way of Life

Steam to Diesel—1836–1960

Though a diesel locomotive cost more than a steam locomotive, running costs
were half as much. ... [Diesels] needed no coal docks, water stations or ash pits
and required fewer people to serve them.*

Life in the Era of Steam

The archival records to which a researcher will have free access are largely
those from the labour-intensive era of steam locomotion. The transition
to diesel engines began in the late 1940s and by the mid-fifties had
dramatically altered the way railways operated. Learning to run a diesel
was relatively easy, but maintenance was another matter and people
who had worked on steam engines became redundant. The change came
quickly and the last regularly scheduled steam-operated train on the CN
ran 25 April 1960. The CPR ran its last steam train on 1 May 1960. A few
Montreal commuter trains lasted a month longer (Leggett, 1973, p. 181).

The advent of diesels radically changed many railwaymen's jobs and
routines. Divisional points no longer determined schedules. If U.R. was
employed in the running trades during this transition, do not be sur-
prised to find the family moving to a larger centre where railway activities were being concentrated. The railway man's life was becoming more
like that of other people.

Younger researchers may find old records of past ways full of unfa-

---

* MacKay, 1992, p. 187.

19

miliar terms and puzzling jobs. Some things have not changed, but many have. Most of those who worked in the days of steam are now retired, though many are volunteers with the Railway Historical Association branches and other railway museums, and some have published their stories. Some are told in *The People's Railway*, Chapter Ten, "Railway People," that is based on interviews with former CNR employees, and provides personal views on the railway way of life. *Canadian Rail* also ran several articles in the early 1990s on "Working on the Railway," such as "Six Decades of Railway Life" describing the career of William Doig Robb, who started as a machinist's apprentice in 1871 and retired as a Vice-president of CNR in 1931 (Vol. 439, March–April 1994). The following notes together with the Glossary may help you reconstruct parts of U.R.'s way of life.

Donald MacKay explains how much of this way of life evolved. Canadian railways modelled themselves on American railroads that in the mid-nineteenth century had themselves borrowed from older industries as well the army, with its tradition of seniority, discipline and semi-autonomous regional operations (1992, p. 7).

There were individual railway police forces. It was the railway companies that controlled time, having organized in the 1880s four time zones across the United States for their operating convenience, with five-and-a-half in Canada.

Trades and Literacy

The railway "Brotherhoods" grew out of the traditions of medieval trade guilds and their "mysteries" that were taught to apprentices by journeymen and Masters of the trade. The Industrial Revolution saw the advent of steam power that required men skilled in more modern mysteries, such as how to build metal boilers that did not explode—at least not too often. The crafts of safely operating a steam locomotive, of building and maintaining cars and locomotives, track, roadbeds and bridges, led to such designations as Master mechanic, Master car builder, Roadmaster. For almost all trades, and certainly for any hope of advancement, the ability to read and write were essential.

Safety

Written train orders were the norm; they were transmitted along telegraph lines, but the train dispatcher's orders started and ended on paper, and north of Mexico, almost always in English. Written records of orders and events were essential in case of an accident. *"I only followed orders, not my fault!"* In the early days of railroading many workers were injured or killed. Brakemen fell off the tops of boxcars while trying to set the brakes, or were crushed between cars they were trying to couple; enginemen and firemen were killed when the boiler blew up, or in collisions. Finally, at the turn of the century, the U.S. Congress passed a few basic safety laws that spilled over into Canada.

Time

In the mid-nineteenth century, when most people travelled by road (horse drawn carriages) or water (steam boats were fastest), Fred Angus reminds us that "where railways were built, average speeds suddenly increased by tenfold." Time became important because although an error of five minutes would have had little significance in a stagecoach or steamship schedule, "on the railway, particularly where trains on single tracks had to meet, such an error could be disastrous." Accurate timekeeping became an important part of railway life, and fortunately, watchmakers were improving their skills and designs and developing the precision instrument that became the official railroad watch.

If you have inherited U.R.'s railroad pocket watch (probably a Waltham), you will want to read Fred Angus's "Railroad Pocket Watches in Canada" in *Canadian Rail* No. 343 (August 1980), pp. 228–247. He tells us that "Canada did not produce railroad watches, but some U.S.-made watches were produced to Canadian specifications, and many other U.S. railroad watches were used on Canadian railways" (p.232)—being American made, they are called "railroad," not railway pocket watches. The CPR had adopted 24-hour time on its Western lines in the 1880s, so watches ordered for the CPR, and later other Canadian railways, had the numerals "13" to "24" on the dial, over or under the usual numbers, or Roman numerals. The stem-winding watch came into common use soon after 1870, so a key was no longer needed. In 1893 in the United States, uniform standards were adopted for railroad watches that included a plain dial with Arabic numerals, so if your railroad watch has Roman numerals it was probably made before that date. Angus gives other advice on dating watches as well as tables of CPR Waltham watch serial numbers with dates.

Seniority

Seniority was a major factor in assigning the jobs of railway employees, not only in the two groups of "running trades": conductors, trainmen or brakemen and baggagemen, and the engineers or engine-drivers and firemen; but also for all the employees at stations, yards, terminals, in maintenance-of-way and bridge and buildings, from section workers to foremen, station agents and telegraph operators.

Within any given category, a new employee started at the bottom of the seniority list, in job assignments and pay. An employee would start as a "temp" trainee and get whatever assignments were left over. There was a "standby list," where available staff were listed for any assignment that came up. Generally, it operated on the basis that anyone who had finished one temporary assignment went to the bottom of the list and worked up it again.

The next step was for the employee to bid for regular assignments (for example, a regular train run from here to there and back) on the basis of his "seniority"—months or years of service. The one with the most seniority would get the assignment. Not surprisingly, the winner might displace someone else, who could in turn displace (bump) a worker lower on the list.

Who wanted what assignment could vary widely. Perhaps they liked passenger trains better than freights, perhaps living in one town better than another, or laying over between runs in places where they had friends or family. Whether on passenger trains or freight trains, railway employees were accustomed to moving to where the job took them. Most had family, friends and contacts to help; everybody knew where to find the boarding houses, cheap hotels and restaurants.

Passenger Operations

In the "Before VIA" past, passenger operations fell into three rough categories: through express trains running across the continent or between major centres (for example, Toronto to Montreal); long-distance local trains that ran between major centres but stopped much more often for local traffic; and local trains, or milk runs, many of which actually did bring milk in the morning from every way-station to a city, taking back the empty milk cans in the evening as they returned to the "away" point. Many of these were also mail trains. The mail car had a mail-slot in the side so while a train idled at a station, loading or unloading milk cans, townspeople could post letters that would be processed en route by the mail clerk.

The passenger and baggage cars on transcontinental and intercity express trains normally stayed with the train for the entire run, although dining and sleeping cars might be added or taken out as required by the service, and on some runs cars would be cut off for, or added from, a connecting sub-destination.

Locomotives on intercity express trains had larger tenders carrying more coal and water. They would stay on for the entire run and, except for major maintenance, would be regularly assigned to the same trains and runs. On transcontinental trains, the locomotives were changed off according to the territory and the train consist (load). The locomotive that crossed the prairies was not suited to the (probably double-headed) haul over the Rockies.

In later times, locomotives ran through several divisional points, but engine crews and train crews normally still changed off at the divisional points, which usually were also watering and coaling points. This meant that these crews were intimately familiar with every bump and jolt in their divisional territory and could tell where they were just by listening to the sound of the track. That was a part of the craft's mystery.

The local milk-run trains were, in a way, the reverse of other railway runs. They would "overnight" at the "away" end of their line, where the locomotive was cleaned and maintained by a "hostler" and the cars cleaned and made ready for the next day's run to the city and back. It therefore made sense for the running crew to live at the "away" end, and these regular runs, with every night at home, were much prized by some of the senior running-trades.

Freight Operations

Freight was somewhat more sporadic than passenger operations, for it depended on traffic and availability of equipment. There were "regular" freight trains between major centres as well as local "way-freights" that picked up and dropped off cars at every sawmill, factory and cattle yard along their line.

As trains became faster, particularly in passenger service, the "mileage" run by crews became more important than actual time worked. A man might do a month's mileage in a week or ten days, then relax at home.

Boarding houses and Bunkhouses

Running crews normally lived at one end of their runs, and except for the "milk-runs," almost always at the divisional point. Running trade crews usually went out one day and (if they were lucky and had the seniority) came back the next.

They had to have somewhere to sleep the night they were away. Freight conductors and brakemen could sleep in the caboose, which tended to be "theirs"; others might stay in a railway-operated bunkhouse or a railwayman's boarding house or with friends or family. They had to report where they would be, so that (until the general availability of telephones) the "call-boy" (usually some railway worker's young son) could find them for their next assignment.

If you are wondering where young U.R. met his future wife, look at both ends of his run, he probably spent as much time in one place as the other. The boarding-house keeper's daughter would be a likely choice. A few senior crew members might live somewhere along the line, where regular train service let them "deadhead" to the divisional point to work their regular runs. They too would overnight at one end of the stint.

Worker Classifications

Throughout the railway hierarchy there was a fundamental division between locomotives and "cars." The Master mechanic was in charge of locomotive maintenance and performance. The Master car builder was responsible for all "cars," both passenger and freight.

Running Trades

Most glamorous were the "running trades": the Enginemen (engineer or driver) and Firemen, made the train run; the other group, Conductors and Brakemen, were concerned with what the train carried, passengers or freight. There was little crossover between these groups because that would mean a major change of trade, different knowledge and loss of seniority. Passenger Service and Freight Service operations also tended to remain separate, at least when seniority gave a man his choice between looking after demanding passengers or dealing with complex freight manifests.

The novice started as a "spare"—fireman or brakeman. Having gained enough seniority, he could "bid in" a regular run in his trade. A fireman would occasionally be allowed to handle the controls (as well as shovelling the required tons of coal) and eventually became a "spare" engineer. Similarly, the brakeman would become a "spare" conductor and eventually a full conductor.

First Class Service

The sleeper, lounge and dining car crews on first-class cars were a special category. Sleeping car crews (conductor and porters) typically stayed with their passengers (to give consistent service and collect their tips) and did not change off with the train crew. Dining car crews (captain, cook and waiters) stayed with their dining car to provision it and be ready for the next stint.

"Pullman Car" was a common term for all sleeping cars. However, in Canada, most such cars were neither built nor run by the American based Pullman Company, but by the individual railways. Pullman served many American lines, and a few minor ones in Canada, so be careful when searching for "Pullman" porters and conductors, records might be with the Pullman Company or with a Canadian railway. "Except for the Grand Trunk Railway (GTR), which employed black cooks and waiters in its dining cars, Canadian railway companies employed blacks almost exclusively as sleeping car porters …" (Calliste, 1987, p. 1).

Agnes Calliste expounds on the lot of the sleeping car porter from a labour union point of view, pointing out that change only occurred after the amalgamation of the dining car and porters' locals of the Canadian Brotherhood of Railway Transport and General Workers (CBRT) in 1964. Her attitude is contemporary, but researchers should remember that if U.R. was a Porter in 1900, or even during the depression years of the 1930s, social mores were not the same as they are now. Both the CNR and the CPR with its associated companies, provided jobs for black sleeping car porters; not great jobs, but regular, steady, respectable work. In Montreal, where a lot of runs began or ended, many established their families in the downtown area, between and west of the two train stations within an easy walk of their work. "Little Burgundy" was a "salt and pepper" district on the eastern fringes of St. Henri as Mairuth (Hodge) Sarsfield, who grew up in this Montreal milieu, explains in her novel, *No Crystal Stair* (1997). Set in the mid-forties, reading her story will bring the black community to life, explain some of the social structure and the resentment and anger that resulted.

The Order of Sleeping Car Porters was organized in Canada in 1918, the Brotherhood of Sleeping Car Porters, in 1925, in New York. CNR porters were unionized but the CPR fought against it and only in 1942 did CPR porters join the Order. A recent book, *My name's not George: the story of the Brotherhood of Sleeping Car Porters: personal reminiscences of Stanley G. Grizzle*, by S.G. Grizzle and John Cooper (1997) gives a Canadian viewpoint. An older study by William H. Harris, *Keeping the Faith: A. Philip Randolph, Milton P. Webster, and the Brotherhood of Sleeping Car Porters, 1925–1937* (c. 1977) offers the American story with little Canadian content.

Canadian railways did recruit in the United States, often bringing men in as transient migrant workers, so their families could not accompany them. Agnes Calliste's paper explains the situation and for anyone researching this segment of railway life, the books listed in her notes are invaluable.

Roundhouses and Maintenance Shops

Roundhouses varied from a simple shed to house the locomotive at the outbound end of a milk run to multi-locomotive roundhouses, with turntables and maintenance shops found at major divisional points.

Repairs that the Division shop could not handle would be sent off to the larger Regional shops.

The hostlers looked after the locomotives once they were in the yard, moving them, dumping the fires and starting them again the next morning, and making sure the engines were oiled, watered and fuelled, ready to run the next trip.

Yard Crews

Divisional points and classification yards would have one or more switching locomotives on duty (with engine crew) and yardmen necessary to perform the switching operations or make up trains. Yardmen were a branch of the brakeman/conductor group. Workers in yard service tended to have a relatively stable home life.

Carmen were responsible for cleaning and maintenance of cars, mostly at divisional points and ends of lines. They checked the lubrication and condition of journal (wheel) bearings that if allowed to run dry would lead to "hot-boxes" and potentially serious accidents. There was also the "car-knocker," who went down an entire passenger train, tapping each wheel with a hammer. The right sound meant a wheel/axle was okay, but if the noise was different, it indicated a potential cracked wheel or axle.

Cleaners, the people who made the interior of the passenger cars presentable for the next day's run, might be women. Except in wartime, this is one of the very few job categories where you will sometimes find women working.

Station Agents and Clerks

In smaller stations, the agent was jack of many trades. He was the telegraph operator who received and transmitted train orders from the dispatcher, he set the signals, sold tickets, received and delivered express and freight and collected and remitted money. Larger stations would have assistants and telegraph operators to handle specific jobs.

Some telegraph operators and agents moved from place to place every few years as they gained seniority and worked up the ladder; others found a place in a town they liked and stayed put. Some agents' wives played an important part in station operations, officially or unofficially.

Maintenance-of-Way

This was the department responsible for maintenance of roadbed, rails, ties, spikes, "ballast" (gravel), switches, etc. The track had to be smooth and level and "shimmed" in winter to cope with frost heaving. Quality of track maintenance varied depending on many factors, but it involved regular inspections and repairs. Each Division or subdivision was divided into Sections, each some eight to fifteen miles in length. Each Section was in charge of a section foreman, assisted by one or more sectionmen. Basically labourers, these men had to live near their work, since there was little transport other than handcars. They often lived in "section houses" provided by the railway; look for their families near small stations and flag stops along the line. At the working level, a Roadmaster working out of Division headquarters was in charge. You can find fuller information with a lot of pictures and early advertisements for special equipment in David L. Davies' "Maintenance-of-Way in British Columbia 1890 to 1980," *Canadian Rail*, Vol. 492 (Jan.–Feb. 2003).

Bridge and Building

The Bridge and Building Department was responsible for structures. Essentially tradesmen, they would normally be stationed at Division headquarters and only go on-site when and where required. Both Maintenance-of-Way and Bridge and Building reported to the Division Engineer. His office was located at the Division office. The "big cheese" for each division was the Division Superintendent, whose word was law, and issued by his Chief Clerk, *he who must be obeyed*.

The Shops

In the early 1850s the Grand Trunk, Great Western and some smaller roads built large car shops, but they originally leased these structures to private contractors who outfitted them to supply large orders for cars. Once the lines were running, the railways first took over the car building, then the more complicated task of building locomotives (Craven and Traves, 1983, p. 255).

Soon car shops and locomotive shops were building, or rebuilding and repairing much of the equipment that made up Canadian trains. Brass baggage racks, wooden and upholstered furnishings, signal lamps, all the bits and pieces might be made in-house, employing skilled craftsmen. The apprentice system trained thousands of skilled workers, and the executives in charge of the Motive Power and Car Equipment branch were usually men who rose through the ranks in the shops rather than from operations and the running trades.

The big railway shops made an enormous contribution to the economy of such cities as Hamilton and Stratford, Ontario, Winnipeg (Transcona), Manitoba, and Moncton, New Brunswick. The Grand Trunk (CNR) shop at Point St. Charles in Montreal covered over thirty acres "with iron foundry, rolling mill, wheel mill, smithy and thousands of boilermakers, machinists, electricians, moulders, pattern makers, pipe fitters, metal workers and carpenters" (MacKay, 1992 p. 7). The CPR's Angus Shops also employed thousands of workers in east-end Montreal. Shop workers were organized in the long-established craft-specific trades and union records may exist for many of these occupations that at first do not appear to be railway-related.

Business Cars and Private Cars

The People's Railway (p.176) explains the subtle distinction: "Traditionally a railway president travelled like a prince in what the public calls a private car and the railways call a business car—private cars being those used by government officials and businessmen like Timothy Eaton."

For railway officials, business cars had the advantage that they could be hooked on to whatever train was going where they wanted to go, left on a siding near the station, and however remote the location, provide office or meeting space, sleeping quarters, a dining room and kitchen with a steward to care for things. The president of the railway, of course, would have a very elegant car or cars, and perhaps a larger staff, but the stewards and other attendants would be railway employees.

In the 1920s the CNR maintained a fleet of eighty such cars: "four for the prime minister and cabinet and two for the governor general, one for the railway commissioners and seventy-three for railway work" (p. 176). However, in the "golden age" of railroads, many wealthy men owned a railway car fitted up to their taste, rather like the private jets of today's rock stars. Their staff might or might not be railway employees.

Brotherhoods, Orders and Trade Unions

The oldest rail labour union in North America is the Brotherhood of Locomotive Engineers (BLE). Originally called the Brotherhood of the Footboard, it was organized on 8 May 1863 at Marshall, Michigan, by Michigan Central engineers. In 1867 the *Locomotive Engineers Monthly Journal* began publication. The brotherhood also created a life insurance service, which was a major factor in union growth.

The Order of Railway Conductors began as a temperance and benevolent society in 1868, the Brotherhood of Locomotive Firemen and Enginemen (BLF&E) was founded in 1873, and the Brotherhood of Railroad Trainmen (BTR) in 1883 (as the Brotherhood of Railroad Brakemen until 1889). This pattern of forming a separate union for each class of employee persisted (Telegraphers, Signalmen, Sleeping Car Porters, etc.), and there was very little co-operation between them in the early days. "International" Brotherhoods crossed the border into Canada, but all the headquarters were in the U.S.A.

The International Brotherhood of Railroad Employees, with headquarters in Boston, took in members from various non-running trades. In October 1908, Canadian members employed by the ICR sent representatives to a conference in Moncton, New Brunswick. It was here that the Canadian Brotherhood of Railroad Employees was born. It was the first national industrial railway labour union. The history of what is now the Canadian Brotherhood of Railway, Transport and General Workers is told by W.E. Greening and M.M. Maclean in *It Was Never Easy 1908–1958* (Ottawa, 1961). Here you will find lists of the many craft unions that they eventually absorbed as well as a bibliography.

Short but informative histories of many railway unions are to be found in Hubbard's *Encyclopedia of North American Railroading*. Many records of the Canadian unions are at the LAC. Once in MG 28, which has become part of Canadian Records Division, you can now search for them on ArchiviaNet.

Special Jobs and Trains

The Railway Mail Service

On 25 Feb. 1872, James Harris & Son were awarded a contract for $6,000.00 to build "Two Postal Cars for Intercolonial Railway" (*Sessional Papers*, [hereafter *SP*] 1878, No. 21, p. 66). From the time the first trains ran until the railway mail service ended officially on 24 April 1971, railroads and the postal service were intimately linked; Station Agents often served as the local Post Master, mail cars were a standard addition to most fast trains and many local trains. Railway Mail Clerks were as much a part of railroading as railway employees, but they were employed by the Post Office Department. If U.R. was a Mail Clerk on a train, don't look for him in railway records.

However, because he was paid by the Dominion of Canada, around the turn of the twentieth century, you can find him in the *Sessional Papers*, in the "Auditor General's Report" on the Post Office where "Superintendents and Railway Mail Clerks: Salaries —" are listed and totalled for every District of the country. They are listed alphabetically, but no place or railways are given, just the postal district. As well, Post Office Department Railway Mail records are in the Archives of Canada in RG 3, E-4. Susan McLeod O'Reilly's *On Track: The Railway Mail Service in Canada* is a fascinating account of this very special world, with many pictures and documents from the Canadian Postal Archives and the National Postal Museum as well as the LAC.

Special Trains

At the Library and Archives Canada web page <www.collectionscanada. ca>, do not overlook the "Kids' Site of Canadian Trains" where one section describes a number of special train types such as: School trains, Silk trains (MacKay, 1986, pp. 131–9), Soldier or Troop trains, Funeral trains, Royal trains and "Odd trains," which included Circus trains, Hospital trains and Ski trains.

If U.R. was ever employed on a royal train or a special funeral train like the one that took the late Prime Minister Trudeau's body to and from Ottawa, that will certainly be part of the family's legends and perhaps best documented in their scrap books or contemporary newspaper accounts.

Rather like the railway mail service clerks, records of the doctors, dentists, teachers and others who took their services by rail to remote communities might be with provincial or other Government agencies, or private companies. Some of the cars of a circus train were specially built and might be owned by the circus. Again, workers might be either railway or circus employees.

Canadian Railway Troops

If U.R. Ancestor served in World War I, he might have been part of the Canadian Overseas Railway Construction Corps, or later the Canadian Railway Troops. By the time the war ended this force reached a nominal strength of almost 15,000. On the battlefields of Europe, from April 1917 until the end of World War I, the Canadian Railway Troops constructed, repaired and operated 1,169 miles of standard gauge, and 1,404 miles of narrow gauge rail lines, which moved ammunition and supplies to the front lines. Particularly if family legends include unlikely sounding tales such as "he drove a train over Vimy Ridge," knowing such units existed can point your research in the right direction.

The service records will be with those of the other Canadian Forces in the Archives of Canada, but the fascinating story of the work this group of Canadian railway men has been told by Fred W. Angus in *Canadian Rail*, No.437 (Nov.–Dec. 1993, pp.191–214), with follow-up commentaries in No.439 (Mar.–Apr. 1994) including a list of the "units of the Canadian Railway Troops, with their dates of organization and disbanding," contributed by R. F. Corley. *Canadian Railway Troops during World War I: The War Diaries* (published in 1995 by Wilson's Pub. Co.) is a rich source of photographs.

Canadian railway employees who enlisted during the Second World War may have ended up with the Railway Operating Unit of the Canadian Army Overseas. Some details of their service, with photographs, was given in the *Canadian Pacific Staff Bulletin*, Nov.–Dec. 1944, and reprinted in *Canadian Rail* No. 449 (Nov.–Dec. 1995, pp. 248–9). Again, service records will be with those of the other Canadian Forces. Library and Archives Canada's AMICUS catalogue also turned up a book by Allin J. Mandar of the Museum Restoration Service, *Line Clear for Up*

Trains: A History of No. 1 Canadian Railway Operating Group, R.C.E., 1943–1945 (1991), also a well-illustrated account.

Railways Didn't Build Railroads

Railway companies did a lot of other things: they obtained charters for the lines they wanted to build, elected boards of directors and obtained financing from businessmen, municipalities, provinces and the federal Government. Having your town on a railway was the late-nineteenth century equivalent to being on a major highway. It was seen as an unrivalled source of commerce and wealth. At the end of the nineteenth century, railway promotion was as serious a form of financial speculation, and as full of risk, as any of the high-tech "dot-com" offerings at the end of the twentieth century.

But when it came to the actual building of the railroad, contractors: big and small, British, American and local did the actual work. In a few cases they were hired by the Government of Canada, usually through the Department of Public Works. Often, however, a big contractor saw where there might be a place for a railway and put the promoters up to applying for a charter. These contractors hired the labourers and teams they required.

Men and Horses

Railroad building before 1900 was not construction as we know it today; there were no bulldozers, graders, dump-trucks or power shovels. Out in the bush or on the prairies, there were few roads or existing railways to bring in supplies. The right-of-way and the roadbed were cleared and graded by work-gangs of men and teams of horses, sometimes based locally, sometimes brought in by the contractors. Iron or steel rails had to come from "outside" and would usually be brought in from one or both ends of the partially completed railroad. Next to the locomotives and rolling stock, they were often the last thing to arrive. In the early years of railroad construction provincial governments sometimes subsidized such work, so every now and then a contractor's payroll or payment vouchers turn up among that Government's records in Government archives. (Not often though.)

On the sparsely settled prairies, local labour and materials were not readily available. Before World War I thousands of men came from the British Isles and Europe to Winnipeg and other points in the West to work as railroad construction labourers. Such immigrants might be indebted to the contractor who sometimes paid their passage. Their names can be found on the passenger manifests for Halifax or Quebec City, but tracking them further west will be almost impossible, unless they eventually homesteaded in the newly established provinces.

Railroad Neighbours

Some of the LAC's recently acquired CNR Legal Department records deal with contracts with railroad neighbours for rights-of-way or crossings. When the railways were originally built, farmers and landowners along the right-of-way might find short-term jobs for themselves, their sons, or their teams of horses. They also had the opportunity to supply and sell cross-ties, as well as timber for the sometimes enormous trestles and bridges. Most of these were initially built of wood, which was available, cheap and short-lived. Once the line was running, if it made any money, these could be replaced as needed with embankments, and steel bridges could be brought in by rail.

Railway Construction Records

If U.R. worked on railroad construction as outlined above, there is a very slim chance that any records of use to you have survived because so many of the nineteenth and early twentieth century contractors were British or American companies. Only if the builder was a local company are records perhaps with some local library or museum. Some payroll records from Mackenzie & Mann exist in the LAC holdings in RG 30 and a scattering of very early payrolls from the Maritimes are found in Government Records because the Dominion of Canada was involved in building some railways.

The Department of Public Works (RG 11) had a Railway Branch that, in 1879, became a separate Department of Railways and Canals (RG 43). The history of these, their activities and responsibilities is described in ArchiviaNet, "Department of Railways and Canals fonds," Railway Branch [MIKAN # 134563]. As well, early *Sessional Papers of the Dominion of Canada* provide quite detailed lists of expenditures for some of the lines that were built by Public Works Railway branch. Even small local contractors may turn up in *Sessional Papers*.

Because the Government was the final authority in determining where the right-of-way ran in many cases, Library and Archives Canada also have a large holding of right-of-way maps that sometimes show the owners of the lands the railways' lines crossed. These are in the Cartographic and Architectural Division (former National Map Collection) in Ottawa, and the inventory is being added to the ArchiviaNet index.

Chinese Labourers

When the CPR was being built, sub-contractors in China or Hong Kong brought contract labourers (sometimes termed "coolies"), to British Columbia, mostly from a few counties in the Pearl River delta in Guangdong [Kwang Tung] Province. These men were not hired as individuals but in large groups, perhaps a thousand men, through agents representing the Six Companies of Kwang Tung. The CPR was built during the period of free entry (1858–1884) when Chinese could enter and leave Canada with few restrictions—and with almost no records. The sub-contractors who hired the men and brought them across the Pacific, usually looked after their food and housing in the construction camps, and were pledged to look after their welfare in North America. They also arranged the return to China of those who survived the accidents (or the scurvy) and chose not to remain.

In ArchiviaNet, in the Government of Canada Files, Department of Transport (RG 12), vol. 2008, among various CPR "Officials and employees" files, is one concerning "Use of oriental labour in construction of Canadian Pacific Railway in British Columbia," 1880–1884.

A number of labour-oriented papers on the Chinese in Canada can be found in *Canadian Ethnic Studies*, Vol. XIX, No. 3, 1987. As well, Pierre Burton's *The Last Spike* includes a detailed description of the Chinese labourers' life, on pages 194 to 206. *From China to Canada: A History of the Chinese Communities in Canada*, edited by Edgar Wickberg, offers an overview of Chinese immigration to Canada and *Across the Generations, A History of the Chinese in Canada* is on the Internet at <http://collections.ic.gc.ca/generations/>.

Originally, employee records were kept in ledgers, but by 1920 most companies had transferred their data to file cards or loose-leaf sheets that were easier to sort, but easier to go missing. Presumably this card, all in the same hand and same coloured ink, was copied from an earlier ledger. Althea's father was given his "back records" card when metal file drawers were being cleared for reuse during the Second World War.

ere They Are

of Records

ced steam locomotives and
.e great era of the railroads
f paper. With the exception
ed by the CNR, hardly any
nicrofilmed. The mountain
nountain.

:d Web sites have local and
al records can be found at
1 Chapter One, "Getting
gitized, that is an expensive,
'ou still have to contact the
To find addresses and other
contact information, go to <www.cdncouncilarchives.ca> where you can
search the directory for the institutions you are interested in. As well,
<www.usask.ca/archives/menu.html> also lists most Canadian archives
with links to Web sites for fuller information.

Make an Appointment

The First Law of Research states that if you turn up unexpected, the
one person who knows about the material you want will be on holidays,
attending a three-day conference in another city, or tied up in "planning

project" meetings for the next four days. Always write or call in advance.

As well, while libraries and museums are usually open on weekends, senior archivists and special collection librarians are rarely available then. Historical associations, staffed by volunteers, may be open for limited hours or *by appointment only*. If coming from a distance, write ahead and plan your research.

Ownership and Public Access

Appointments are essential when dealing with private companies. Records are the property of the companies that generated them and, except for the CNR, who turned theirs over to the National Archives of Canada with a thirty-year closure, and a few provincially owned lines, private companies have no obligation to allow the public access to their records. Moreover, these days few can afford the staff time to conduct historic research in files that are almost certainly stored in some remote warehouse. Many today, including the giant CPR, politely refuse to answer genealogists' queries.

It Will Take Time

Most repositories require you to register and obtain a pass on your first visit. In most cases this must be done during business hours, on weekdays and never on statutory holidays. Some, including Library and Archives Canada, require a piece of official photo-identification (passport, driver's license), or several documents with your full name and address, for the first registration.

Library and Archives Canada stores many books and most records outside its public building in Ottawa so you must allow at least a full business day or more for retrieval. This can also be the case elsewhere; another reason to plan your visit in advance.

Do not count on being able to have anything copied mechanically.

Railway records can be bulky, in heavy binders, and often very fragile. Very few are available on microfilm or microfiche (from which printouts can be made safely). "Safely" refers to the safety of the records, not yours; you will be expected to wear light cotton gloves, handle things with care, use pencil only and never mix up the order of documents in a file.

Records Managers, Archivists and the Luck of the Draw

In the 1960s, faced with those mountains of paper, records managers and archivists identified three types of records: legal and business files that must be kept permanently, others with a shorter useful life that could be shredded after a certain length of time and the rest that were to be weeded from files and destroyed. A few old ledgers *might* be relegated to the company library.

Where company archives were set up, it was to assist the public relations department and one or two historians writing corporate histories. Thus they preserved the legally essential documents and enough posters, ephemera and "interesting old stuff" to mount a good display. Some also kept samples of older non-essential files, to show "how it was done." When selecting among case files they might use the one-file-in-a-hundred approach.

As a result, most company archives contain all Board minutes, lists of stockholders, deeds, leases, and other legal and financial documents, but may have only a small sample of operations and staff records. Government archives hold the files of correspondence of politicians and bureaucrats with developers, promoters and some builders. These are rarely of any genealogical use unless U.R. was a top executive.

Where to Look

If U.R. was with the ICR & PEI Railway in the early years, the *Sessional Papers of the Dominion of Canada* (1868–1925) may tell you all you need to know. If with the CGR and CNR before the 1950s, there is a good chance he is mentioned in surviving records at Library and Archives Canada. However, these have come to light and been released to the Archives of Canada only in the past decade or two. Many are old and fragile and they have not been microfilmed. Most, eventually, will be added to the General Index database. Access is restricted by the 30 year closure limits, and researchers may have to secure special permission. If U.R. was with other CNR companies, you might find something at the LAC in RG 30 though most records are original payrolls, with a few surviving ledgers and lists.

If U.R. was with a CPR affiliate, you are limited almost entirely to published material. Most CPR personnel records remain with the pension division and are not accessible. However, some staff records have turned up in regional archives and museums (*see* Chapters Four and Five).

The same is true of other independent railway companies. The Ontario Northland has closed down its archives and, being a provincial organization, the staff records are subject to Ontario's Privacy Act. These laws make archivists and personnel management very cautious. However, for both CNR and CPR staff, there are trade union records, both at the LAC and in smaller repositories.

Libraries, Museums and Cataloguers

Genealogically useful documents, like seniority lists, often survive in a railway enthusiast's collection or among personal papers, and will turn up in manuscript collections at some museum, historical association or research library. Such surviving records will usually be indexed by the name of the railway company that generated them. That may mean only the name of the company as it appears on the documents, but if the cataloguer knew railway history, it could include interim corporate owners.

Records with Genealogical Information

Personnel Records

From very early times, most railways kept records of their employees: when they joined, where they worked, how much they were paid, as well as every promotion and raise in pay. Most include date of birth, some list next of kin, religious denomination, even physical appearance (helpful information when identifying and dealing with bodies in a wreck).

Company Service Records

In the nineteenth century most such records were kept in special ledgers by clerks who wrote a fine copper-plate script. The ledger may or may not be divided alphabetically; in either case entries tend to be chronological. The clerk would often make an index to the entries, itself probably chronological within the letter of the alphabet.

After the turn of the twentieth century, staff service records were often transferred to large index cards, or typed on printed forms and filed in heavy-duty binders. Each time the format changed and information was transferred to a "new and improved" system, the old records were at risk. This could happen when companies merged or offices moved. Old ledgers may be forgotten in a closet, but cards tend to disappear so the drawers can be used for something else. Today computers have taken over but never underestimate the garbage-in garbage-out factor in data entry.

Staff records might be kept by the local sub-division, at Regional headquarters, or both. Often an employee number is the access key. Most staff records were, or are scheduled for destruction, but a basic service record fact sheet usually ends up with the pension department.

Seniority Lists

Because they were something individual workers were vitally interested in and unions and brotherhoods kept a sharp eye on, seniority lists turn up in many collections of railway memorabilia in both museums and archives, all across the country. Finding one or two will confirm U.R.'s job status and Division. Finding a collection of them covering a number of years may trace his whole career.

Benevolent and Pension Funds

Benevolent or provident funds might be company or union sponsored, and their records tend to survive, at least for a time. Many were actually more than pension funds; they made provision for work-related injuries and provided for early retirement under some circumstances. Where board minutes survive, cases might be recorded in detail. When an employee retired, pension payments were often noted and sometimes the executor who received the last payment is identified. A few indexes, organized by employee or pension number, have survived and access may depend on knowing U.R.'s pension number. A pension number just might be recorded in some family papers, so keep an eye out for such information.

Insurance Association Records

In the early years of railroading, many workers could not buy life insurance because there was too great a chance of their being killed. Workers, perhaps encouraged by insurance agents, formed associations to secure insurance. In fact this was one factor in the early unionization of railway employees. Certificate and/or beneficiary registers can supplement family information in Service records. Ledgers might be kept by local secretaries as well as the associations' general secretary. Such volunteer work for unions and insurance groups might well be done at home, after hours. As a result, such material can turn up among private papers in libraries and museums, in estate sales, in second-hand bookstores—almost anywhere.

Pay Records

> … normally, I'd recommend the destruction of payrolls after 15 years, and their microfilming only in the most exceptional circumstances. –John Andreassen in a letter dated 17 November 1996 (LAC RG30, at one time filed with the Finding Aid for Deposit #40)

Payrolls

The enormous bulk of these records (CN's Atlantic Region alone generated over fifty feet a year) means that only statistical samples survive, say two months out of every four or five years, and hardly any after the 1930s. A few from smaller CN lines survive in RG 30 on microfilm, while others are there only in their original form.

A payroll search is a Catch 22 situation. The facts you must know to find the entry are the facts the entry will give you. Payroll records tend to be large printed sheets, one or more as necessary for each group and sub-group of workers. These are usually bound together in large volumes. A small company might put all the sheets for a specific time period in a single volume. Large operations will separate volumes by Division, by type of work, as well as by time period. The number of volumes will vary.

Some such volumes in LAC's RG 30 (CNR) are identified by type of work or Division, so if you know what U.R. did and where, you might find how much he was paid. If two or three hundred volumes covering ten or fifteen years are unidentified, the researcher has little hope, though it is an excuse for a long visit to Ottawa.

Time Books

Time books usually come in pairs, covering alternate months. While one book recorded hours worked, the other was used to make up payrolls. It was customary (and with the CPR well into the 1940s) to be paid a month in arrears; that is your time worked was entered in the January/ March/etc. book, and at the end of the month the time book went off to payroll, being replaced by the February/April book. The workers were paid for January's time at the end of February, for February at the end of March, and so on. Accessing individuals is difficult and may depend on knowing the employee's number, sometimes a time clock number. These numbers could change.

Stock and Bond Records

Employees might be eligible to purchase company bonds. A ledger listing sales, often by instalments deducted from pay, is a corporate record and so has probably survived. Selling War Savings Certificates or War Bonds, again by pay deductions, might be a volunteer service in offices or Divisions. Like the group insurance associations, such work could be done after hours at home, so records can turn up in strange places.

Labour Union Records

After World War II (c. 1946) the records of the United Transportation Union (LAC MG 28) contain a number of individual grievances, seniority claims, disability and other case files. The inventories rarely name names, rather they refer to "Member Lodge 221, Sarnia." If you know where and when U.R. might have filed some complaint, the full story might be in some general chairman's files. Union records also include some seniority lists. An active union member might turn up as a correspondent or lodge officer in the lodge files.

Pictorial Records

Libraries, art galleries, museums and archives of all sizes have collections of prints, pictures and photographs. Most are catalogued by subject, and some also by creator (photographer or artist). Try looking under Transportation—Land/Ground—Railway/Railroad, then by company name.

One trick is to check the illustration credits in books you have found relating to your particular Railway. Sometimes the writer will say what collections they are from or who created them. This may point you to holdings in small local collections, or give you the name of some photographer or artist whose *fond* may produced other pictures.

Local museum or library collections will tend to have illustrations from the region. The enormous collection of illustrative material at Library and Archives Canada is no longer divided between the Photography Collection and the Picture Division; it is now all within the Art and Photography Division. Remember the prints and engravings from the nineteenth century. *Canadian Illustrated News* 1869–1883, for example, printed over 15,000 illustrations, and these are indexed at the Archives. As Library and Archives Canada fully integrate their collections of illustrative material, it should become easier to locate other less common pictures as well.

Check local libraries and museums for motion pictures (amateur or professional) and audiotapes from oral-history projects. At Library and Archives Canada, in the Audio-Visual Division, you can find the collections of the National Film Board (CNR associations), Associated Screen News (CPR associations) and several other broadcasting company collections, as well as CBC material. Do not overlook architectural drawing and maps, at the LAC they are in the Cartographic and Architectural Division and gradually being entered in ArchiviaNet.

In addition, major collections of illustrative material are found at the Metropolitan Toronto Library; McCord Museum, Montreal; New Brunswick Museum, Saint John; Royal Ontario Museum (Sigmund Samuel Collection), Toronto and the Glenbow Institute, Calgary.

Four

Library and Archives Canada

Holdings - RG 30/R231

In the Beginning

The first company to run a train in Canada was the Champlain and St. Lawrence Rail Road; incorporated in 1832, it opened on 21 July 1836. With time, it became a part of the Montreal and Champlain Railway which in turn became part of the Grand Trunk Railway which was absorbed into the Canadian National Railway Company. Thus the earliest surviving corporate records of a Canadian railway are in Library and Archives Canada, a small part of a Government Record Group, for many years designated as: RG 30. Today it is called the "Canadian National Railway Company fonds," is renumbered R231 and includes 2,087 metres of textual records.

The old RG 30 was divided into series and smaller sub-series in a perfectly logical system in which RG 30 was followed by Roman numerals indicating the component Systems' groups. These were subdivided using capital letters, then split into numbered series that could be subdivided using lower case letters. For example: RG 30-IV-A-1-e. Alas, 1990s computer software did not readily sort such a mix of numbers and alphabets; computerizing catalogues demanded a sortable numbering system. This has been developed and is now coming into use.

Archivists, however, do not willingly discard any element of the past, so "RG 30" lingers on in the real world, particularly for Maps, Architectural drawings and Graphics—and on kilometres of storage boxes.

At the present time RG 30 (R231) is not governed by the Access to Information and Privacy Acts, but is subject to a collective agreement made with Canadian National that sets a thirty-year closure limit. If there is a valid reason to access any document less than thirty years old, special permission must be obtained from CN. The person to contact at CN can change, so ask the Reference Archivist in the general Researchers Services Division (main desk in the Reference Room, third floor) to obtain the name and address of whoever is currently responsible for granting permission.

A CNR Family

If U.R. Ancestor was born much before 1900 and retired from the CNR (after 1960 CN), he could not have worked for that railway system "all his life." The CNR did not exist until after the First World War. U.R. probably started with the Intercolonial or the Grand Trunk or J.R. Booth's much smaller Canada Atlantic Railway or perhaps the Canadian Northern Railway. There was also the short-lived Canadian Government Railway. The CNR was incorporated on 6 June 1919 but had been operating under the name Canadian National Railways since 20 December 1918. Over the ensuing years, CN "evolved from nearly 700 separate companies, the majority of which had operated independently under their own names" (*Towards CN*, 1972, p. 5) and these include subsidiary operations (steamships, hotels, radio and telegraphs, etc.) that are not directly concerned with running trains. A major component of the CNR was the Grand Trunk Railway that was absorbed in January 1923 (Leggett, 1973, p.132).

Over the years, these companies produced a mountain of records that by 1960 had become a problem to store and access. John Andreassen (1909–1991) came to Montreal in 1962 to serve as System Archivist, and was instrumental in having older records placed with the Public Archives of Canada. The agreement to transfer the CNR's historic records was dated 28 January 1963. John Andreassen, however, was a records management expert; he believed in keeping only "representative samples" of obsolete documents, and, according to my notes from a course in Archives and Records Management given at McGill University in 1965–66, his concern was for scholars preparing corporate histories, not genealogists and family historians.

Archival Descriptions Change

The "arrangement and content" of RG 30, "Records of the Canadian National Railways 1836–1975" are concisely described in *Government Archives Division* (1991, pp.52–4). It then occupied 1,540.4 metres of shelf space, with 1,208 reels of microfilm; few of which are of any value to genealogists.

The "Canadian National Railway Company fonds" (from 1836 into the 1980s with more still to be released), new Number: R231-0-0-E [MIKAN no. 95], is described and itemized in the "General Index" of ArchiviaNet, and starts with a concise history of the administration of CN up to its privatization in November 1995. The entry includes a list of the new numbers assigned to various RG 30 series and sub-series. Until the catalogue is completely computerized, researchers will have to think in two modes, shifting between older holdings in RG 30 and new accessions in R231. It is probably safe to use the RG 30 classifications for the original CNR holdings and any accessions predating about 1990. However, for later CN accessions in ArchiviaNet, it may help to understand the principles and terminology behind the new system.

In 1990, the Bureau of Canadian Archives issued *Rules for Archival Description*. This was an enormous undertaking that started when professional archivists first confronted computers and realized they needed standardized ways to enter data. "*Fonds*" and "Series," "files" and "items" are the terms these Rules advise for use with "true archives" and these are the terms you can expect to encounter.

- *Fonds* is now used for large basic units, although **RG** and **MG** numbers will persist until those kilometres of boxes are relabelled.

- **Series** remains the second level of sorting or description. Both RGs and *fonds* are broken down into **Series.** This may be as far as a descriptive guide goes. A Series used to be broken into sub-series; now it usually contains a number of **Files** (sometimes in file folders or perhaps bound ledgers).

- **Files** in turn hold **Items,** perhaps one or two, possibly a hundred or more. "File lists" may be made if time and money permit, giving the title of each **File** folder within a "series." File titles usually offer a good indication of what may be found within. However, if some long-ago clerk mis-labelled the folder or misfiled items, the file-titles can be totally misleading.

- **Items** are rarely inventoried individually except for the most important materials, such as a Prime Minister's correspondence.

- **Volume Number** (usually meaning box number), is really the vital fact you must have to actually secure a file or item. Always write it down.

Electronic Finding Aids

These days at LAC, researchers will be directed to the computerized catalogues. The Library's is AMICUS; the Archives' is ArchiviaNet. The professional consultants at either Reference Desk will show you how their system works and with a little practice you can bring up entries of what you want, there or at home on your own computer. The Library's catalogue is more or less complete, though new acquisitions arrive daily and have to be added. ArchiviaNet is still a work in progress. Every time you use it you will find something new has been added and something familiar has been changed. There is no point in describing what is there today because it will be different tomorrow.

A Few Tips

- **MAX is Your Best Friend**. Every time you start a new search, make sure to change the "Number of Entries Displayed" from 12 to MAX. MAX will give you 200 entries, enough for most searches, though some Finding Aids contain thousands more.

- **Write down *all* numbers**: both new numbers and old numbers, any Volume or File numbers that are given, and the "MIKAN" number.

- **MIKAN Number and AMICUS Number**. These are unique numbers assigned to each item in the LAC catalogues. Once you have found an item that interests you, you can use these numbers to quickly find exactly the same entry again, MIKAN No. in the "General Index" of ArchiviaNet, AMICUS No. in AMICUS (Library).

- **Arrangement Structure**, in ArchiviaNet, for some large *fonds* like R231 [MIKAN No. 95] at the top, at the end of the heading toolbar is a block or button labelled "Arrangement Structure." When an entry has this, click on it for a second level of description and numbers.

Location of CNR Fonds

RG 30 (now R231) is part of the Government Records Branch [GRB], and at present the archivists have their offices in the West Memorial Building, directly across Wellington St. from the main Library and Archives building. Both Wellington St. buildings are in desperate need of renovation so they expect to move to Gatineau (formerly Hull) across the Ottawa River, where the actual boxes of documents are now in modern climate controlled storage in a new building.

> *What is written here will change. Expect construction, closed off areas, and always check in advance as to hours and places. Researchers will probably be accommodated at the Wellington Street building, but you must allow at least one full business day, or better yet thirty-six hours, for retrieval.*

Plan your research with these limits in mind. Except for a few payrolls of subsidiary companies, no personnel-related material is on microfilm and you can not pop in and have a quick look.

That's not quite true, as I learned when an archivist asked "Have you ever looked in the *Sessional Papers?*" You can pop into the Library Reading Room where, at the east end on open shelves you find bound volumes of the *Dominion of Canada Sessional Papers*. In these, for the most part in the Reports of the Auditor General, is an amazing wealth of personnel information on anyone who was paid by the Government from the 1870s until the mid-1920s. The Department of Railways and Canals operated the Intercolonial and Prince Edward Island Railways, and a few other small lines. How to use this source is detailed beginning on page 66.

When You Arrive

As 395 Wellington St. is renovated routines may change but researchers should obtain a Research Pass to Library and Archives Canada on the ground floor of the main building. First time registrants may be asked for photo-identification, but once you are in the computer you are part of the research family.

Next, sign in at the Commissionaires' desk, obtain a locker key and store your coat and any large bags. The Commissionaire will give you a clear plastic bag if you want to take your laptop with you. Then go to the third floor where the Reference Room is on your right as you exit the elevator or stairwell. If you are a family history beginner, talk to the people at the Genealogy Desk. They have a binder with a great deal of information on available railway data and will start you off in the right direction.

If you are an experienced researcher, have done your homework, but have a specific question relating to RG 30 (R231) or other Government records, ask the Reference Archivist at the main desk. The archivists in the Researchers Services Division will show you how to use both the printed and electronic finding aids and, if your question stumps them, will help you set up a consultation with the archivist in charge of whatever records you require, be they Canadian National (RG 30), Department of Railways and Canals (RG 43), the Canadian Transport Commission (RG 46) or others.

The old-but-still-useful Inventory Lists to the various Government Record Groups are kept on open shelves in the Reference Room. They are in blue ring binders and RG 30 fills two binders where you can study the original arrangement and find some 1990s accession lists at the end. However, since about 1995, these lists are no longer being updated and new accessions are found in the electronic indexes in ArchiviaNet. Red ring binders contain the Inventory Lists to the MG records, where you will find labour union papers, and the same caveats apply.

Inventory Lists and Volume Numbers

The original Inventory Lists to RG 30 provide a brief outline of the history of each company and how it links into the CN family. It then identifies what records of each company have survived, and gives volume numbers. The volume numbers bear no relation to the logically organized Inventory Lists, whose letters and numbers identify the individual document series. *However, volume numbers are essential. Write them down.*

The contents of RG 30 did not arrive at the National Archives drawn up in marching order by company and type of record. Rather, they arrived piecemeal by box—or by boxcar, and later in small bundles found when an office moved. The archivists dealt with these various lots of papers by assigning a "Deposit number," then, as each deposit was inventoried, dividing it into numbered "Volumes." RG 30 was originally stored and identified by these volume numbers and the detailed finding aid file folders were labelled with the deposit numbers and associated volume numbers.

- **Finding Aids:** RG 30 was among the early fonds inventoried using the computer. When this started, computer memory was limited and database fields were small, so most are "Computer generated lists sorted by Volume number, listing Volume number, file number, file title and inclusive dates," on accordion folded sheets. Some are still on paper, and if large, are not very user-friendly. Those that have been incorporated into ArchiviaNet are readily searchable in the "General Index" (use keyword to search) or "Government of Canada Files" database. In this, use the "Detailed Search Screen," enter the Finding Aid number in the appropriate box. Be sure to limit your search using appropriate keywords, and always change number of entries displayed to MAX (200).

- **The Volume number is essential for retrieving documents.** Write it down.

Organization of RG 30

The records are organized into six "System" series (see page 62). These series were sub-divided by component "groups," some artificially created in order to rationalize the inventory of holdings. Ultimately, there was a unique document series (numbers and letters) assigned to every corporate predecessor and subsidiary of the CNR of which the Archives holds records, identified under its corporate name. The contents are largely corporate business documents such as minute books, cash books and ledgers, lists of stockholder and traffic and equipment registers, and rarely include personnel material. Many files titled "Personnel" turn out to be rules, agreements or pay schedules.

The following list includes those records that may be of use to genealogists and family historians. They correspond to entries in the blue RG 30 inventory binders; volume numbers and some contents have been checked where possible and editor's notes added. New accessions are listed separately following the old inventory, and here you must start thinking R231.

RG 30—Arrangement and Content	R231 number
I Grand Trunk System	R231-41-3
II Central Vermont Railway System	R231-997-0
III Canadian Northern System	R231-998-2
IV Canadian Government Railways System	R231-755-9
V Canadian National Railways System	R231-0-0 [numbered by Series]
VI London Port Stanley Railway Co.	R231-553-8

Where new numbers have a final letter: E = English; F = French

FA = finding aid, "electronic" available online, "paper" on shelves west of the Archives reference desk

RG 30 I A Grand Trunk Railway Co. 1846–1936

Series 5 - b. General manager and president's office

NEW ii Letter Books 1897–1911 (vols. 1781–1793) FA 30-17 (vol. 1781)
Letter Book 35, Charles M. Hays letters:

SEE 15 November 1898 (pp. 517–522) list of Audit office (Montreal?) staff increases; interesting because quite a few women employed.

4 January 1890 (p. 575–577) lists each new employee in several Divisions and each increase in pay.

Copies of these letters have been made available to the LAC Genealogy Desk.

Series 8 Records Relating to Personnel

NEW Vols. 2937 and 2935 (a & c below), name lists have been indexed (by surname) by the LAC Genealogy Desk and may include age and date of entering service.

   a. (vol. 2937) Permanent Staff Register 1886–1913, FA 30-36

36 pages - about 150 names of men employed at the Middle Division Toronto. Now indexed, ask at Genealogy desk.

   b. Payrolls, 1862–71; 1889–1921

   (vol. 1752) N. & N.W. Div. 1892–93

   (vol. 1886) Maintenance - Island Pond to Portland, 1906–07

   (vols. 2032–2058) Steam ships & special units, 1900–1905

   (vols. 7095–7285) payrolls 1915–1917

   (vol. 10786) payrolls [no finding aid, no date]

   (vols. 14400–14433) see new accessions on page XX: MIKAN No. 47523

   c. (vol. 2935) Staff Records, Toronto Office 1913–1914. 55 pp. [Now indexed, gives date of birth, ask at Genealogy desk].

   d. (vol. 2838) Staff Time, Traffic Auditors Office 1892–1896

Series 9 Operational Records

   d. Staff Records: re Provident funds 1874–1878

   (vol. 2943) large ledger with reports, actuarial estimates and accounts of Provident Fund. Lists 54 names of employees wishing to add years, gives ages and service data.

   (vol. 2944) large ledger listing payments made from 1 Apr. 1875 to 25 Feb. 1878.

This chronological list (by date of payment) records payments to Doctors and/or employees (from all across the system) with voucher numbers. *Not Indexed*, virtually unaccessible.

Series 13 Pictorial records (d.) and Maps (e), see FA 30-38; 30-42; 30-49. Each company's associated photographs and cartographic records (maps and drawings) are held in the appropriate LAC collection.

RG 30 I E Grand Trunk Pacific Railway System 1900–1959

Series 1 f. Personnel Records

   i (vols. 1114–1115) Roll Books 1908–1912, FA 30-14

lists attendance at various meetings, signatures

Note that for all practical purposes, any large payroll (e.g. 200 ± volumes occupying 20+ metres of shelf space) is inaccessible unless the contents of the individual volumes are identified at least by geographic location (Division, Section) and job categories or types of operations.

ii   Payrolls 1906–1920 (26.7 metres) FA 30-44

        (vols. 6833–7023) Winnipeg Office, 1906–1916 (262 vols.)

        (vols. 7024–7051) Branch Lines (various)

        (vols. 7052–7053) Prince Rupert Engineering 1906–1909

        (vol. 7056) Special Military Payrolls, 1914–1920

        (vols.7061–7062) Passenger Department, by Division, 1916

iii   (vols.1838–1840) Unclaimed Wages 1905–1912, FA 30-19

Series 2 Grand Trunk Pacific Branch Lines Co., 1906–1934

        (vol.1835) Unclaimed Wages record 1909–1912, unindex.

Series 8 Grand Trunk Pacific Development Co. Ltd. 1903–1942

        (vols. 7057–7060) Payrolls for 1909–1916

Series 10 Grand Trunk Pacific Terminal Elevator Co. 1907–1937

        vols. 7054–7055) payrolls for 1907–1908

RG 30 I F Great Western Railway System 1835–1960

Series 1 London and Gore Railroad Co.

b.   Operating Records 1854–1888

        (vol.928) Car Dept. pay lists, Oct. 1860–Aug. 1862

RG 30 II A Central Vermont System

Series 2 h. Personnel Records

i   (vol. 2098) Washington agreement with Unions 1936

ii   (vol. 14431) Officer's payroll 1939–1953

RG 30 III A Canadian Northern Railway Co. Ltd 1898–1956

Series 7 Records relating to Personnel

a.   (vol.3005) Seniority List 1917

b.   (vol. 3138 - envelope 20) List of Employees, Winnipeg 1912

2 pages handwritten on printed forms, signed.

c.   Payrolls [FA 30-44, by date only]

        (vols. 7067–7068) Payrolls, general, 1901–1911 (2.0 m.)

        (vols. 6533–6832) Payrolls, Winnipeg Off. 1902–1916 (30.0 m.)

        (vols. 7087–7091) Payrolls, Winnipeg Term. 1912–1916

d.   (vol.3134) Service record - V.L. Hansen, Engineer, 1918

RG 30 III B Mackenzie Mann & Co. 1896–1916

This company is *not* a railway, but built and sometimes operated the Canadian Northern, also active in Nova Scotia.

Series 1

a.   (vols. 2484–2525) Payrolls 1902–1919

(vol. 7063) Payrolls 1916

RG 30 III E Canadian Northern in Ontario

Series 2 James Bay Rail Road Co. 1903–1906

(vol. 929) Payrolls 1903–1904

RG 30 III G Canadian Northern in British Columbia

Series 1   (vols. 7064–7066) Payrolls 1914–1916, one year per volume. See FA 30-44.

RG 30 III H Canadian Northern in Nova Scotia FA 30-40

Series 1 Halifax and South West Railway Co., 1901–1939

(vols. 6135–6137) Payrolls 1914–1915

(vols. 6231) Payrolls 1916

RG 30 IV A Intercolonial and Canadian Government Railway and Predecessors 1868–1931

Also consult the post 1990 Accessions at the end of these RG 30 Series Lists, and see "Sessional Papers," p. 76.

Series 1 Intercolonial and Prince Edward Island Railways

e.   Operating Records

iv   (vols.12456–58) Casualty Records 1877–1901 , microfilm C-13447 to 13448, FA 30-85

g.   Personnel Records FA 30-23; 30-40; 30-126

As well, an older, more detailed finding aid is in the Genealogy Desk railway ring binder. These sometimes provide some information on the dates, locations and types of jobs you may find in these various volumes of payrolls. Many are place-specific. See also recent accession item 4, MIKAN No. 49221 below. **Note:** Fuller information is available in the Genealogy Desk railway ring binder.

i   Paylists & Payrolls, general 1891–1916 (4.2 m.)

(Vols. 2081, 6141–42, 6144, 6151–53, 6159–62, 6169–73,

6179–6182, 6186–93, 6196–229, 6232–37, 6239–54, 6256–59; 14511–14515).

ii (vols. 6145–50, 6154–56) Payrolls, Prince Edward Island Railway 1908–1916 (0.3 m.) FA 30-40

iii ICR and PEI Railway Employees, history of employees and Provident Fund membership 1855–1910 (Vols. 14962–14974) FA 30-126 (electronic). Registers nos. 1 to 12.

Note: these ledgers were in accession 92-93/215, boxes 303 to 315.

Series 2 European and North American Railway Co. 1859

(vol. 8553) Payroll [misc.] and invoices 1859

Series 3 Nova Scotia Railway Company 1856–1858

(vols. 2067 & 8553) letter books and payrolls 1856

RG 30 IV B National Transcontinental Railway 1905–1924

Series 1 (vols. 6133–34) Payrolls

Book I May 1913–June 1915

Book 2, July 1915–Dec. 1915

(vols. 6183–84) Payrolls: Track 1910–1915; Stations 1913–15

(vols. 6158, 6174–75) Payrolls: Track 1915

RG 30 IV C Government Acquired Railways in N.B. FA 30-40

Series 1 Canada Eastern Railway Co., 1891–1903

(v. 6119–6120) Payrolls, 1891–1903

Series 2 International Railway Co. of N.B., 1911–1913

(vol. 6185) Payroll 1911–1913

Series 3 New Brunswick & Prince Edward Island Railway Co.,

(vol. 6117, 8259, 10337) Payrolls, Jan.1909–July 1914

Series 4 Salisbury & Albert Railway Co.

(vol. 6137) Payrolls - 1918

RG 30 IV D Government Acquired Railways in Nova Scotia

Series 1 Inverness & Richmond Railway Co., 1906–1924

(vol. 6143, 6163) original Payrolls, Jan.–Dec. 1916

Microfilm only: M 1681–1684, Payrolls Feb. 1906–Mar. 1924.

RG 30 IV E Government Acquired Railways in Quebec

Series 5 Atlantic, Quebec & Western Railway Co., 1907–1916 (vols. 6131–32) original Payrolls, 1916

Microfilm only: M 1694–1714, Payrolls 2 Jan.1915–30 Sept.1929.

Series 6 Quebec Oriental Railway, 1913–1916

(vols. 6122–30, 6177–78, 6194) original Payrolls, 1913–1916.

Microfilm only: M 1740–1795, Payrolls 18 June 1910–2 Jan.1929.

Series 8 Temiscouata Railway Co. 1886–1949

(vol. 6164, 6255) original Payrolls, Jan.–Dec. 1916

(vols. 6165–68) original Payrolls, 1896–1914

Microfilm only: M 1715–1739, Payrolls 31 Dec.1889–15 Jan. 1949.

RG 30 IV G Newfoundland Railways, 1881,1884,1904–1946 (0.1 m)

Records include a pay book, photographs, timetables.

RG 30 IV H Northern Alberta Railways 1909–1954

(vols. 8521–8522, 9739, 9768, 9773, 9785, 10377) general operations. Records of predecessor companies on Microfilm: M 3245–3259. Originals at Archives of Alberta (pre 1 July 1929) for: Edmonton, Dunvegan & B.C.Railway Co.; Alberta & Great Waterways Railway Co.; Central Canada Railway Co.; Central Canada Express Co.; Pembina Valley Railway.

C N R 1922–1995

RG 30 V A Canadian National Railway

Series 1 Office of the President

(vol. 10647) is a 122 p. index to Donald Gordon's personal scrapbooks. Originals at Queen's University, available on Microfilms M-1968 to M-1971.

Series 7 Personnel and Compensation Records

a. Rates of pay, NO individuals named

b. Employee Compensation Statements, NO Individuals named

c. Labour Relations: 5280 files, individual cases with Unions. FA 30-82, Listed by case number, gives date and Brotherhood, no personal names.

e. (vol. 2151) Regulations and memoranda relating to re-employment of employees after WW II Service.

f.   (vol. 11708) Employee Bond Subscription, 1929–1930.

Headquarters and St. Lawrence Region[?] employee purchases of CNR Bonds, some alphabetical by first letter of last name, but also sections for various Departments. No family data, difficult to access individuals without knowing exact job.

g.   (vols. 14404–14425) Officials and Supervisors salary payrolls, 1923–1942, FA 30-123

i   (vol. 14428) Changes in Official Positions, titles, salaries, effective 1 Sept. 1932; 1932–1933.

Series 9 Headquarters and Departmental Records

[*See also* new accessions item 3, MIKAN No. 49220, p. 73]

g.   Legal Department Records (Western Region) 1920–1954 (vols. 4725–4729) index in vols. 4725–4729. FA 30-39

These records deal mostly with land and right-of-way leases and legal matters, but quite a few files concern legal dealings with named individuals.

h.   Legal Department Records (Central Region) 1905–1926, FA 30-51

(Vols. 8559–8660; 8671–8898; 8999–9244; 9256–9587; 9612; 9658–9664) Index in Vols. 9658–9664, Microfilm reels C-4625 to C4629.

Finding Aid 30-51 is a searchable electronic database. Use the "Detailed Search" screen, enter 30-51 in the Finding Aid space and try various keyword searches (with wild-card ?) such as "injur?, personal," "death?," personal names or place names. This will bring up claims by individuals.

i.   Superintendent's Records, Southwest Ontario Subdivision 1909–1962

(vol. 2551) daily operations GTR/CNR between Black Rock, N.Y. and Windsor, Ont. Subdivision office was in St. Thomas.

j.   Public Relations Department, 1863–1981

(vols. 14434–14441; 14449–14510; 14516–14537; 14773–14780; 14805–14878).

(vols. 14773–14780) Biographical material on high-level officials.

This can be searched by individual's name, using ArchiviaNet, Government of Canada Files, Finding Aid number 30-18.

k.   Radio Department 1923–1943 (*see* p. 26))
(microfilm reels M-537, M-538, M-584, M-715) Further records are found in the E. Austin Weir fonds, new number R2327-0-5-E [old number MG30-D67], MIKAN # 119846.

Series 13 Records of Individual Officers

d.   (vols. 111926–11949) Col. G.R. Stevens, research papers and notes for his History of the CNR.

If you know someone was interviewed or mentioned, there might be additional material somewhere in these 23 volumes.

RG 30 V B CN Subsidiary Companies 1898–1962 (35.3 m)

Note: This is where records of CN's Express, Merchant Marine, Steam Ship, Telegraph, Terminal and Hotel operations will be found.

Series 17 CNR Road Department, Southern Ontario, see R231, MIKAN 158442 below.

RG 30 VI London and Port Stanley Railway 1856–

Series 6 Pay and Personnel Records

b.   (vol. 13009) Time Book, 1 July to 31 August 1915

Bound ledger with name of each employee, hours worked, wage rate and total for each day and pay period.

c.   (vols. 12983–12990) Payrolls (½ month), incomplete for 1917, 1920, 1925–30, 1933, 1935, 1938–39, 1941–42
(vols. 3051–3052, accession 1995–96/102) Payrolls (½ month), same dates as above, see FA 30-91, 30-128 chronological box-lists.

d.   (vols.130012–130019) Payroll Transfer Ledgers [daily time records used to make up payrolls] 1941–1950, 1956–1957. FA 30-107 contains no further information.

e.   (vol. 130020) Earning records cards and sheets, 1958. (see c.above)

f.   (vols. 130021–130022) Time Distribution Ledgers, 1926–1935

Ledgers record hours worked by each employee, duty involved, pay earned etc. by month. FA 30-107

Series 7 Reports and Records

m.　(vol. 6279) Accident report records 1940–1949

A record book in which accident reports were summarized.

Genealogical Sources in R231

First Ask the LAC Genealogy Desk

Because so many people worked for Canadian railways, and their descendants want more information, the Genealogy Desk at the LAC (third floor) has compiled a ring binder on Railway Records, many of which have arrived at the LAC since the first edition of this book was compiled. New discoveries are being added regularly; so do ask them what's new? Some of their discoveries include:

RG 30 W-1995–96/111 CNR Winnipeg Staff, employees 1918/1926–1977

boxes 1-75 Much of western Canada, numerical by employee number

Held in Winnipeg regional centre LAC, contact: David Horky, Archivist, GARDD - Winnipeg Office, Manitoba Regional Record Centre, 1700 Inkster Blvd., Winnipeg R2X 2T1 (204) 984-1469

R231 1999-00455-8 MIKAN 158442 old number RG 30-V-B-17

Personnel service records of the CNR Road Department, Southern Ontario, consists of one register of form 182-B arranged alphabetically, with two A–Z series. This is a very thick register that cannot be photocopied. It must be viewed on-site. Check ArchiviaNet for details of contents.

New Accessions in R231

The archivist presently responsible for R231, Michael Dufresne, has identified eleven recent accessions that might have information useful to genealogists. The first includes the then-unprocessed accession (92–93/215) we were able to look at a decade ago, the rest of the items on this list are new. Most of accession 92–93/215 was processed and added to various appropriate Series in the RG 30 lists above, so you will find some overlaps. We have attempted to cross-reference these, but be aware that this is the confusing mid-point in the shift from RG 30 to R231.

1. Central Administration of Canadian National, Montreal 1862–1988

MIKAN No. 46111 includes former ACCESSION 92–93/215 GAD [GAD = Government Archives Division]

Use the MIKAN number to find this in the "General Index" of ArchiviaNet. It comprises 144 metres of textual records spanning well over a century. Electronic Finding Aids exist for only a portion of the accession, these numbers are listed in the ArchiviaNet entry, as are former archival reference numbers. To use the Finding Aids, use the "Government Records" Detailed Search screen, which has a space for "Finding Aid Number." Limit your search using keywords, and remember MAX is your best friend. Details and some sample pages are available in the LAC Genealogy Desk's railway ring binder.

FA 30-130 lists some 15,000 files relating to land development and farm contracts, presumably relating to subsidized settlement of individuals or contracts for right-of-way etc.

UPDATE: accession 92–93/215 had just arrived at the NA when the first edition was in preparation. It had not yet been inventoried but we were privileged to look at likely sounding items (boxes). We listed the Numbered Boxes that contained personnel records that vary from "of some interest but difficult to access" to "fabulous—but very fragile." To locate this material, researchers can use the old accession number and the box number, which now seems to be the *item* number. See new accession item 8 (MIKAN no. 133097) below where some of this is explained. FA 30–124 covers boxes 1 to 50 only.

Regarding the ICR & PEI Railway

Some of the following records cover most employees in the Atlantic Region (Maritimes plus Quebec to Rivière du Loup), or those who started in that region, from around 1879 to about 1947. The records contain a wide variety of genealogical information and are often interrelated. However, this interrelated material has come to light over a number of years in several different accessions, and the best we can do is try to cross-reference the newer discoveries. Be sure to consult the LAC Genealogy Desk, and as well, check wage and salary lists in *Sessional Papers.*

Boxes 241 to 250

ICR & PEI Benevolent Fund Board Minutes, 1907–1959, typescript in post-binders. Each binder has mss. index of individual cases considered by the board. Concerns both early retirement for health reasons and at age sixty-five.

Box 252

ICR & PEI Benevolent Fund Voucher Register A–G. Relates to boxes 241–250 above. March 1931–±1957. Books for H–Z are missing.

Box 251

CNR in New Brunswick — possibly Temiscouata Railway — Staff service records: pay and promotion, 2 binders: IN SERVICE and OUT OF SERVICE, 1910–1950, individual sheets, alphabetical [appears to have been started about 1919 but we have been unable to locate it in ArchiviaNet in 2004].

Box 255

Originally titled "Mackenzie & Mann Pensions." Now recognized as CN Headquarters, Public Relations files and Pension Dept. files. One file of Senior Officials' Pension Applications from 1950s. Arranged alphabetically and cross indexed.

Boxes 282, 283 & 479

ICR & CGR Employees' R & I [Recreation and Insurance] Certificate and Beneficiary Registers, 1890–1914; 1914–1918; ±1931/35–Dec.1947. Alphabetical by first letter of last name. Not Indexed. See item 8 below which is the register for 1918–1938 (MIKAN No. 133097).

Box 288 to 300

Grand Trunk Point St. Charles Car Shops Workmen's Time Books. There ought to be two vols. per year, alternate months, but some are missing. Point of access is employee NUMBER [for mechanical time clock system?] No Index or Staff list gives NUMBER. Individual's number sometimes changes over time, making access rather difficult.

Boxes 301 & 302

ICR Staff Record Books, Index vols. Physical condition very poor. Essential for accessing individuals in Staff Record Books.

Boxes 303 to 315

ICR Staff Record Books, 1879±–1910±, large ledgers probably started around 1883, last entries after 1911. Physical condition very poor. See above IV-A-1-g-iii.

Box 316

Canadian National Railway Service Record 1922± to 1950±. Unidentified sub-divisions east of Toronto. Not indexed but alphabetical by first letter of last name, a lot of personal information, some give physical appearance & next of kin.

2. Canadian National Railways [related to payroll]

MIKAN No. 47523 [not yet in ArchiviaNet] Finding aid 30-123, paper.

Former ref. RG 30, Accession 1994–95/732 GAD, added to RG 30 I-A-8-b

(vols. 14400–14433) Grand Trunk Railway & Subsidiaries, officials salary payrolls 1915 to May 1923.

(vols. 14404–14418) CNR, officials' salary payrolls, May 1923–1939.

(vols. 14419–14425) CNR, supervisors' salary payrolls, 1933–1942.

(vols. 14432–14433) officials of CN Steamships, Telegraph, etc.

(vol. 14428) Changes in officials positions, titles, salaries, 1 Sept. 1923 [when GTR was absorbed into CNR].

3. Miscellaneous Records 1839–1982

MIKAN No. 49220 18.9 metres of textual records, described in ArchiviaNet.

Former reference RG 30-V-A-9 [CNR Headquarters and Departmental Records, listed under CNR above], accession 1996–97/1083 GAD. Finding aid is electronic 30-18. **Note** there is a variety of very miscellaneous stuff here. The finding aid, 30-18 is online and also available as a very long computer printout. It is alphabetical, by subject. It can be checked on ArchiviaNet in "Government of Canada Files" database.

Use the "Detailed Search" screen, enter 30-18 in Finding Aid box, and limit search using appropriate Keyword. Be sure to change number of entries displayed to MAX (200).

This is the accession that includes Director of Public Relations files with editorial biographies of many railway executives (1918–1981), for details see above RG 30-V-A-9-iii.

4. Employees provident fund of the Intercolonial and Prince Edward Island Railway, 1907–1959

MIKAN No. 49221, in ArchiviaNet, Finding aid 30-24, paper.

> Part of R231-755-9-E & 755-9-F Canadian Government Railways. Former reference RG 30-IV-A-1-g, accession 1996–97/1084 GAD

Railway employee service record cards in 117 boxes, filed numerically by the employees Provident Fund number. No alphabetical index of employees, but see boxes 241–252 above and item 8 below. Finding Aid 30-24 lists the employee numbers in each box. Details are available in the LAC Genealogy Desk's railway ring binder.

5. Certificates and beneficiary registers of Provident Fund - Canadian Government Railways, 1918–1950

MIKAN No. 133053, in ArchiviaNet, Finding aid, open, 30-144 paper (box-list giving vol.#, file #, file title & inclusive dates). Part of R231-755-9-E & 755-9-F Canadian Government Railways. Other accession no. 1997–98/458 GAD

Three CGR Membership Certificate and Beneficiary Registers. Organized numerically by members' provident fund numbers 91-2000; 17150–17499; 50000–54999; 70000–89999. Includes "tombstone information" (name, occupation department, name of beneficiary, relationship and address).

1936 Grand Trunk Systems Register of pensioners, divided into sub-sections by GT Systems affiliated rail lines, express and telegraph companies, etc. Includes names, home address, pension rate and amount paid during calendar year 1936. Samples of some of these documents are found in LAC Genealogy Desk's railway ring binder.

6. Employees' records of earnings of the Newfoundland Railway - Accounting Department, 1946

MIKAN No. 133055, in Archivianet, Finding aid, open, 30-140 paper.
Other accession no. 1997–98/431 GAD

A register of employees' (alphabetical) bi-monthly/monthly earnings, gross annual wages, taxes deducted for the calendar year 1946. May include address, sex, number of dependents.

7. Accounting ledgers of the Accounting Department, Prince Edward Island Railway, 1881–1913

MIKAN No. 133075, in ArchiviaNet, Finding aid, open, 30-142 paper.
Other accession no. 1997–98/434 GAD

Included is a register of unclaimed employee wages (1861–1906).

8. Membership/beneficiary register of the Employees' Provident Fund of Canadian Government Railway, 1918–1936

MIKAN No. 133097, in ArchiviaNet, Finding Aid, open, 30-141 paper.
Other accession number 1997–98/433 GAD

One register (No. 3), listing employees who were members of the ICR/CGR Provident Fund, 1918–1938, alphabetically arranged. This ledger is one of three [or four?] that serve as the index to the individual Provident Fund member cards, item 4. above (RG 30 acc. 1996–97/1084). Registers numbers 1 and 2 are items/boxes 282 and 283, RG 30 acc. 1992–93/215. Item/box 479 in this same accession may be the volume covering ±1935–Dec. 1947. Details are available in the LAC Genealogy Desk's railway ring binder.

9. Agreement of The Grand Trunk Railway Company of Canada, 1859–1930

MIKAN No. 136006, in ArchiviaNet, Finding aid, open, 30-106 paper
Other accession no. 1997–98/451 GAD

Contains some employee-related records such as

- Salaries paid to GTR foremen and clerks of the Locomotive and Car Departments (1859–1910)

- Semi-annual returns of GTR accident and casualty lists, June 1858 to Dec, 1864.

- CNR Southern Ont. employee service records, ca. 1910–1930. Alphabetical, with personal information relating to pension eligibility, occupation, includes Belleville, Kingston, Coburg, Trenton, Toronto and Niagara Falls. See LAC Genealogy Desk's railway ring binder.

- Also contracts for provision of various goods (for example, firewood) and services, construction, repairs etc. 1859–1877 [may name local suppliers, casual labour etc.]

10. Employee service records of London Car Shops, 1920–1960

MIKAN No. 137365, in ArchiviaNet, no Finding aid. Other accession no. 1997–98/453 GAD

Three ledgers with copies of Employee Service Records, ca. 1920–1960, for the former London Car Shops, London, Ontario.

11. Records of the Office of the Secretary, ca. 1938–1967

MIKAN No. 140811, in ArchiviaNet, no Finding aid. Other accession no. 1997–98/534 GAD

Correspondence files pertaining to subjects such as pensions and superannuation.

Other Sources at the LAC

At Library and Archives Canada, railway-related records are not all in R231 (RG 30). To start with, the books and periodicals you will want to consult are held by the National Library and to find these use the AMICUS catalogue. Other Government records that may hold information on railways, their operation and employees include the Department of Transport (RG 12), Department of Railways and Canals (RG 43) and Canadian Transport Commission (RG 46). Railway-related material can also be found in the Canadian Records Division (formerly Manuscript Division, where numbers started with MG), as well as the Cartographic and Architectural Division, the Documentary Art and Photography Division and the Audio-Visual Division.

Dominion of Canada Sessional Papers

However, if U.R. worked for any Government-run railway like the ICR or PEI, between 1868 and 1925 you would do well to start in the Library of Canada Reading Room where you will find a wealth of personnel material in a most unexpected source.* Would you be interested in a "Statement showing names, occupation and salary of all persons except ordinary mechanics and labourers who were in the service of the Intercolonial Railway, on 31st March, 1876"? Suppose you knew this list included everyone's age? (*SP*, 1878, No. 21, pp. N2–N13.)

On the second floor, at the east end of the main Reading Room there are several stacks of shelves holding bound volumes (orange or tan) of *Sessional Papers of the Dominion of Canada*, issued annually by the Queen's/King's Printer in Ottawa from 1868 to 1923. After that year they are continued in part by the *Annual Departmental Reports*. You will find the full bibliographical data in the National Library's AMICUS catalogue <www.collectionscanada.ca> where you can search either the title or use the AMICUS number: 15507306.

According to AMICUS, they have been microfilmed (by both Micromedia and Princeton Microfilm). They ought to be found in some provincial Legislative Libraries and older University Libraries because the first edition of "the annual reports of the various departments of the Government of the Dominion of Canada" states that this new series "is intended to meet the needs of institutions, chiefly in the nature of Legislative and University Libraries, which in past years had received copies of these reports under the title of 'Sessional Papers.'"

However, they are non-current government serial publications, unlikely to be on the open shelves, and finding them in library catalogues may be tricky. Moreover, each year's papers fill a number of bound volumes.

Volumes within Volumes

Each year's papers have a Volume No.; those issued in 1868 cover the "First Session of the First Parliament of the Dominion of Canada, Session 1867–8" and are Vol. 1. Ten years later, 1878's papers are Vol. 11 [eleven]. However, each year's Volume of *Sessional Papers* comprised

---

*   When I told him we were preparing a revised edition of *Canadian Railway Records*, the archivist Glenn Wright said "Look in the *Sessional Papers*, in the 'Auditor General's Report.' You'll find a lot of railway material you can use." Please join us in saying "Thank you, Glenn Wright!"

"several cloth-bound volumes of approximately equal bulk, the number of reports to a volume being determined by the size of the respective reports." The arrangement of papers or reports varies slightly over the years as bureaucrats "improved" things.

Each year's papers can fill up to a dozen bound books, so within Volume 11 (1878) there are eleven separate volumes/books also numbered. In citations we have standardized "Vol." to refer to the year, "vol." to refer to the various cloth-bound volumes within a year's papers.

Determining which vol. you want in any year's papers can be difficult without actually having at least one vol. in your hand. Fortunately, each *Sessional Paper* is assigned a number. Some Papers are under a page long. Some can fill two or three bound volumes. To find something, you must know the year and the paper's title or number. There are *no nominal indexes*.

Subject Index

At the front of each bound book (vol.) within any year (Vol.) there is a "List of Sessional Papers … Arranged Alphabetically." This is a simple subject index, giving the number of the paper. It is arranged alphabetically, and there is some repetition, so in 1875 (Vol.8) you find: "Accidents, Railways …. (No. 54)" as well as "Railway Accidents …. (No. 54)." Related subjects may be found in different papers, for example, in 1867–8 (Vol.1) we find:

> Railways, Statements of … (No. 13)
> Railways, Indebtedness … (No. 61)
> Railways in Dominion … (No. 73)

Contents of Volumes

Following the subject index is a "List of Sessional Papers … Arranged Numerically and in Volumes." This is essentially a Table of Contents, listing each bound volume (vol.) by number, with a list of the papers it contains. The numbers of the papers are in the left margin so are easy to locate and there is both the name of the paper and a brief summary and sometimes a note "[*not printed*]."

You look in the subject index, find "Railway Accidents … (No. 54)," turn to the Table of Contents pages, see that paper No. 54 is in vol. 8

with many other papers, and learn that it is *not printed*. What one hoped would be long lists of railway accidents is instead one brief paragraph, just the expanded title.

On the other hand, "Railways in Dominion … (No. 73)" is a Return that lists all railways, when built, length, cost of construction and equipment, cost per mile, number of passengers per mile per year, passenger receipts per mile per year, and the same for freight. There is also information on railways under construction (*Sessional Papers*, 1867–8, vol. 9, paper no. 73).

Large papers, like the "Auditor General's Report," can fill more than one book, and they are divided into sections, with each section assigned a number or letter of the alphabet. Each section is paged individually, starting with page 1. These longer papers often have their own subject index but these can be frustrating because the sections are rarely indicated, only a page number is given. The first page 54 you come upon may not contain the subject you expect to find there. Keep hunting, remembering that much of the material is organized more or less alphabetically.

Rather surprisingly, the railway employee information is found in the annual "Auditor General's Report," which after the first few years is usually Paper No. 1, and bound in the first volumes. It can fill as many as three books. The Auditor General's report is arranged alphabetically, so normally in the last volume you will find the Railways and Canals department, "Details of Expenditures and Revenues," following those of the Post Office and just before the Royal Northwest Mounted Police.

Look for the section on "Working Expenses," for U.R.'s railroad. In the volumes for 1909, which deal with 1907–1908, the Intercolonial Railway's operating expenses included "Wages, Moncton Office" as well as wages paid at the "Locomotive Shop" and the "Car shop." Every employee is listed, in the Office by department, giving name, position and annual salary. Workmen in the shops are listed alphabetically, giving the hours they worked, their hourly rate and total paid to them over the year. In the Locomotive Shop, my grandfather, William McCoy, boiler-maker, earned 27¢ an hour for a total of $687.42 between April 1907 and March 1908. For comparison, the General Manager of the ICR earned $6,000.00 and his Chief Clerk, $1,800.00 (*SP*, 1909, No. 1, pp W223, W201).

Even if U.R. did not work for a Government-owned railway, a look through one of these lists will give you a sense of the complexity of running a railway and a feeling for the hierarchy and how working groups were divided. It is also a wonderful guide to salary levels and consequently the buying power of money for any point in time.

Not every audit lists every employee at the Moncton shops, some years only the aggregate wages are given, but the lists do included everyone in the smaller regional shops, every Station Agent, every [telegraph] Operator, and all the clerks and stenographers in the offices. In 1918–1919 I happened on the entry for my aunt Gladys (G.M. McCoy) who was stenographer to the chief medical officer in Moncton, paid for two months at $65.00, three months at $70.00 and seven months at $90.00 (*Sessional Papers*, 1919, No. 1, p. W-228). That same year, on p. W-229 I found my father's pay was increased from $175.00 to $205.00 a month in April. Another curious entry lists under "operations" the cost of "Travel of Officials." Alphabetical, by surname, this list turns up officials with the same name like my father G.E. and his cousin C.L. McCoy who were in different departments, in different cities (pp. W215–W217).

The *Sessional Papers* are not easy to use, but if you can find a run on open shelves where you can look through a year or two of volumes and get a sense of how they are organized, the wealth of data on individuals paid by various arms of the Dominion Government is mind-boggling. These *Papers* are where you find complete lists of "Superintendents and Railway Mail Clerks: Salaries" from British Columbia to Prince Edward Island in the Auditor General's report on the Post Office expenses.

Accidental Deaths

There are also lists of accidental deaths, but these turn up in various reports. For example, the early phases of the survey for the CPR were paid for by the Government and I happened on a list, in Appendix K of Sessional Paper No. 20 in 1878, listing "Lives lost in connection with the Surveys, during the Years 1871, 1872, 1873, 1874, 1875, 1876, 1877 and 1878," giving date, often place and usually cause of death of 38 men including 5 Indians "name unknown" (lost in forest fires). Most of the surveyors drowned or "Broke through ice."

Canadian Records Division

The former Manuscript Division (MG), now called the Canadian Records Division, is where the records of non-government organizations and the papers of private individuals will be found. Search on ArchiviaNet in the "General Inventory," using keywords to limit the number of finds. Among the most useful records for learning more about your U.R. are certain files in the collection of Labour Union papers (MG 28):

MG28, I 215 - Canadian Brotherhood of Railway, Transport and General Workers

> Finding aid no. 774 (40 pp.) provides file lists for vols. 1–91.
> Accession 1995/0061, boxes 1–86 and box 89 restructured, see binder. Microfilm M-3199. There are some restrictions so it is best to consult an archivist.

This Canadian union began in 1908 with a small group of ICR non-operating employees in Moncton, and over the years grew to include bus, tram, taxi, truck, canal and the CN and CP Hotel workers. Most records concern certification, agreements, various union business and conference records. A thorough study of the Finding Aid may turn up specific material related to individual research; the following material is typical of the files that may name names:

> **Vol.22** Death Benefits, Protection Fund, Applications, Lists for contributors 1921–1925

Death Benefit Association List, 1925

> **Vol.58** Death Benefits, Protection Plan, Case Records 1925–1958
> **Vol.59** Directories of Officers 1950–1954
> **Vol.78** Miscellaneous Material, Twenty Year Service Records, 1929–1952
> **Vol.83** Seniority Lists, St.Lawrence and Atlantic Region, 1958, 1963–1966.

MG 28, I 216 - United Transportation Union

> Finding Aid no. 1004, vol.1 (121 pp.) is a file inventory list; vol.2 (194 pp.) is photocopies of the Unions' card file Subject Index, with an index to subjects on pp. 146–149. Be sure to consult the "In Process" lists [MG 28 I - 216] for new accessions, most of which have now been restructured. Consult the binder at the Genealogy Desk.

This Canadian Union was formed in 1969, bringing together four operating unions founded in the United States late in the nineteenth century: The Brotherhood of Locomotive Firemen and Enginemen [BLF&E] (founded 1872), The Brotherhood of Railroad Trainmen [BRT] (founded 1883), the Order of Railway Conductors and Brakemen [ORCB] and the Switchmen's Union of North America. Researchers should read with care the introduction to the Inventory Lists that outlines how the Union functioned.

The BLF&E records, 1886–1974, comprise the bulk of the holding (25.9 metres); the BRT, 1897–1971, is smaller (6.2 metres). The majority of these concern general agreements, rules, regulations and their interpretation and are non-specific as to individuals. However, individual case files will be found in the General Chairmen's records. In particular, the General Chairman, C.N.R. (Central) files include the following for the 1940s–late 1960s (dates vary):

Vol.80 Seniority Lists [restructured]

Vol.83–89 Pay Claims, 1940–1967

Vol.89–90 Discipline Appeals

Vol.91 Complaints

Vols.92–93 Seniority Claims

Vols.94–95 Disability Case Files; Lodge and Seniority Files

Note: individuals are not named in Inventory Lists, only the Lodge number is given. A few files of the Canadian Railway Board of Adjustments give names.

Other Canadian Records (Manuscript Groups)

MG 27 Papers of political figures, 1867–1950, contains railway-related material, usually about promotion, construction, subsidies etc.

MG 30 and 31 "Manuscripts of the first half of the Twentieth Century" and "Manuscripts of the second half of the Twentieth Century" is where you will find such *fonds* as that of Thomas Charles Young (b. 1870, Jasper Alberta), CNR employee, MG 30 (D 66) Originals, 1923–1953. Six inches of assorted material related to railways and western Canada.

R5500-0-6-E (MG31-A 10) *Andrew Audubon Merilees fonds*

One name that will come up again and again is Andrew Audubon

Merrilees (1919–1979) whose collection of material relating to transportation (documents, published works and serials, ephemera, artifacts and photographs) is now at Library and Archives Canada. This important collection was donated to the National Archives of Canada, but when the NA transferred their historical collection of published material to the Library in 1995, the "in print" portion became the "Merrilees Transportation Collection" and is held with other special Library collections. To access the full collection researchers will have to consult both ArchiviaNet and AMICUS. While there is little material relating to individuals, the collection of ephemera and pamphlets, as well as photographs of railway equipment, buildings and people is extensive.

Government Records Relating to Railways
[other than RG 30]

Although you will be directed to ArchiviaNet for your searches, you should also consult the *General Guide Series - Government Archives Division* and read about how these Government departments developed and changed.

RG 3 - Records of the Post Office Department (1799–1987)

Here you will find the Records of the Railway Mail Service and Postal Inspectors, but for lists of Railway Mail Clerks see *Sessional Papers* (p. 76).

RG 12 - Records of the Department of Transport (1787–1995)

Under the classification "Surface" will be found records of railway subsidies, railway lands, buildings, railway charters, and railway track construction. Plans and drawings are in National Map Collection.

As more and more inventories of Government records are added to ArchiviaNet you can expect all sorts of interesting sounding file titles to pop up. As we mention in Chapter Four, LAC holds records of early surveying and planning of the CPR, however, as the Department of Public Works, Railways Branch, was changed into the department of Railways and Canals (RG 43 - 1879) and then became the Department of Transport (RG 12 - 1936), it maintained considerable control over Railway operations, even of private companies such as the CPR and its affiliates. As a result, curious bits of information turn up in the files of RG 12.

There are some files with information about personnel:

vol. 610, accidents - collisions and derailments, see Chapter Six

vol. 2007, file 3606-6, Officials and employees - Canadian Government Railways, 1870–1880

This file contains some lists of appointments to positions with the Intercolonial and Prince Edward Island Railways, including name, occupation, and sometimes date of birth, residence and length of service.

vol. 2007, file 3606-5 Officials and employees - Canadian Pacific Railway Construction, 1879–1884

Lists of names of people employed by the Government during the construction of the CPR, such as engineers, brakemen, clerks and servants. Details include name, occupation and salary.

vol. 2008, file 3606-7 to 3606-17

Files relating to senior executives such as Sir Sandford Fleming, David Pottinger and Frederick Braun, with one file on "use of oriental labour in construction" of the CPR in British Columbia. For details of these files use the "detailed search" screen in the "Government of Canada" database; enter "12" in the Record Group box, 2008 in the Volume Number box. Some, like "Payment of hospital expenses for Canadian Pacific Railway employees treated in St. Boniface, Manitoba, 1876–1880" are probably correspondence relating to company policy, but might include names.

Most of these RG 12, Vol. 2008 files are essentially correspondence files. Just how much detailed employment information, or actual lists of names you might find in them is problematic. It takes time to call up records, wait for their delivery, and then don white cotton gloves and read through a file folder that may hold 25 or more items. Think of it as a "lucky dip" game and decide if you want to play.

RG 43 - Records of the Department of Railways and Canals (1791–1964)

Only Section A: Railway Branch Records 1867–1936, relates to railways. There are few operations and no personnel records, but see Chapter Six on wrecks.

RG 46 - Records of the Canadian Transport Commission (1890–1966)

Consists primarily of formal proceedings and correspondence. Some records of accidents in Series C-II-1 (Central registry Files), see Chapter Six.

Graphic, Photographic and Audio-Visual Material

Cartographic and Architectural Division

This division has absorbed the former National Map Collection and added a wealth of architectural material. Here you will find not only maps and plans of cities, showing where railways ran, but survey plans, track sections, and the architectural drawings for many stations and other railway structures. Over 30,000 items from various RG and MG series are included.

The Map Collection's numbering system, however, does not necessarily follow that used in the RG and MG document inventory lists. Some are based on accession numbers, so ask for help in converting from the document inventory lists. Remember that much of the railway material is in remote storage and can take twenty-four to thirty-six hours for retrieval. The good news is that more and more of the inventory is being added to ArchiviaNet, where searching—and finding what you want—will be much easier.

Art and Photography Division

This collection holds all illustrative art and photographs, in whatever medium and from whatever source. It is easy to overlook the LAC's extensive collection of drawings, early prints, water-colours and posters showing trains and stations, but these can be a source of illustrations for a family history.

The LAC holds part of the CNR photography collection; some came with various archival accessions in RG30, others as a collection of early negatives mostly on nitrate stock, some of which self-destructed. Ask an archivist for help to find out which negatives still survive; I once saw a finding aid consisting of ring binders with photocopies of the hand-written CNR finding list, but when I asked about it this year no one knew about it. Later photographs, kept by the CNR until it was privatized, have been transferred to the Museum of Science and Technology, and part of this collection has been digitized and can be searched on the museum's Web site. However, at the LAC, look in the card index for "transportation - land - railways" as a "subject" and it will turn up pictures in all kinds of other collections. The National Film Board and Photothèque collection contains quite a number of railway photos, as do the Merilees fonds.

If a photograph has ever been requested and a copy negative and print made, it will appear in the general Subject Index cards (with the negative number) and if you find what you want you can order a print quite easily. However, there are many large collections that are rarely delved into. Only one or two pictures among several thousand might appear in the index. In particular, several defunct newspaper photo morgues (*Montreal Herald*, *Montreal Star*) are found here. Remember that for every photograph printed in a newspaper, there are probably five or six or more that have never been seen since the editor rejected them and they were put in a file in the morgue. Read any instructions you can lay your hands on, ask for help and persevere.

Finding what you want may be a matter of luck. As I write this, the Subject Card Index is on the third floor, main building, at the west end of the Archives Reference Room. Ask first at the general reference desk, but through the door and down the west corridor you will find a desk and a consultant with a computer who may be able to advise you about how to order up unindexed material. It helps if you do your homework. Know what you want to find: the company, place, subject. Check related histories and other railway books and note the names of collections and the names of photographers.

Photographers Matter

The LAC holds the files and negatives of a number of commercial photographers, as well as many amateurs. Photographers matter because of copyright; their names are almost always included in catalogue information if known. Thus, their name can serve as a keyword. Where one picture exists, there are probably more, so it may be worthwhile to look at the full collection, not just accept the one print in the index.

Audio-Visual Division

This Division holds material from both CN and CP Systems as well as most other Canadian film, television or broadcasting companies, private and public. Starting in the 1920s, many promotional films were made by the larger railways to encourage tourism. As well, during World War II, the National Film Board made at least one film showing the railways' contributions to the war effort. Ask at the main reference room desk where this division is located this month, and when you find them, ask for help in finding what you want.

GIVEN LIFE PASS—George E. McCoy, assistant chief of car equipment, Montreal, is seen receiving the president's letter of congratulations and good wishes, and life pass, from S. F. Dingle, (left), vice-president, operation, on the occasion of his retirement after more than fifty years of service. On the right is E. R. Battley, chief of motive power and car equipment, who, on behalf of the staff in the mechanical department, presented Mr. McCoy with a matched set of travelling bags.

GREETINGS SWAPP
by W. G. Brinton,
successor, M. B. Ki
at a presentation
who served the co
wallet and scroll
C.N.R. commenced

G. E. McCOY RETIRES

A working career, stretching over more than half a century, ended in Montreal on January 31 as G. E. McCoy, assistant chief of car equipment, retired under the pension rules of the company. For the past eight years, Mr. McCoy has assisted in the preparation of specifications and plans for new and converted equipment and in supervising the maintenance of more than 115,000 freight and passenger cars. Before leaving his office, Mr. McCoy received a leather-bound scroll and a matched set of travelling bags from his associates in the mechanical department, the presentations being made by E. R. Battley, chief of motive power and car equipment.

S. F. Dingle, vice-president, operation, handed Mr. McCoy a letter of congratulations and good wishes from Donald Gordon, C.M.G., chairman and president, and,

the age of fourteen by joining the I.C.R. as mechanical draughtsman's apprentice. After serving as draughtsman, he transferred to the Canadian Government Railways in 1914 as assistant chief draughtsman and, two years later, became assistant master car builder. In 1918, Mr. McCoy joined the C.N.R. as master car builder and, in 1923, was named superintendent of car equipment, Atlantic region. Five years later, he was promoted to general superintendent of car equipment and, in August, 1932, was transferred to Toronto as assistant general superintendent of car equipment, central region. Mr. McCoy was appointed assistant chief of car equipment for the System at the beginning of 1943, with headquarters at Montreal.

The supply men — executives of the railway supply industries — tendered a dinner to Mr. McCoy on his last working day. At the request of the supply fraternity, Mr.

CONFERENCE HON
general freight cla
given a testimonial
Conference, freight
roads. Mr. Gilmo
behalf of the Con
Railroad, toastmas
New York Central
station service, Del

"IKE" WANNA
REACHES RETIRE

Employees of
district rail a

Retirement at 65, "under the pension rules of the company": George E. McCoy, born 8 January 1886, retired 31 January 1951. The account of his retirement, with those of a number of others, appeared in *Canadian National Magazine*, March 1951. Seen here receiving the president's letter of congratulations and a lifetime pass from vice-president S.F. Dingle.

Five

Records in Other Repositories

CPR Records

The purpose of keeping archives is to preserve and make available documentation that is valuable to the company for administrative, legal, promotional and other uses. Records are also collected with the general public in mind and the needs of future generations *for information on the role of the company in Canadian history.*

That quotation is from the explanatory notes the Canadian Pacific Archives once sent to enquirers. The italics are ours. The CPR's role in Canadian history is briefly set out with interesting pictures on the Internet <www.cprheritage.com>. Here it outlines early difficulties, then describes how the company grew into more than just a railway.

… CPR got involved in land settlement and land sales as early as September 1881. CPR erected telegraph lines … transmitting its first commercial telegram in 1882.

In 1882 it also acquired the Dominion Express Company. The CPR started building some of its own steam locomotives as early as 1883 and by that year had CPR steamships on the Great Lakes. It chartered ships on the Pacific Ocean in 1886, launched its own Pacific ships in 1891, got into paddle wheelers in British Columbia's interior in 1893, and on the British Columbia coast in 1901. It expanded to the Atlantic Ocean in 1903. As early as 1886, they tell us, after Van Horne suggested setting up a national park system in the Canadian Rockies, the CPR went into the hotel and tourist trade.

… CPR even discovered natural gas on the Prairies, although quite by accident. In 1886, while digging an artesian well to get water for its steam locomotives, CPR crews stumbled across natural gas in what is now Alderson, Alberta.

After a century of expansion, the economic and business changes in the last decades of the twentieth century forced the CPR to rethink its organization. On October 3, 2001, Canadian Pacific spun out into five separate companies: Canadian Pacific Railway, CP Ships, Fairmont Hotels, Fording Coal and PanCanadian Energy. PanCanadian has since merged with Alberta Energy Corporation to form EnCana Corporation.

Canadian Pacific Railway Archives

The Canadian Pacific Archives hold a large and fascinating collection of documents (or copies of documents when the originals must be kept secure in vaults) relating to corporate history: rail, hotels, airlines, ships, natural resources, communication. If you visit their Web site, researchers wanting "Historical Information From Canadian Pacific" are told:

> The Archives, an internal department of Canadian Pacific Railway, provides fee-based services at the discretion of the company. Any commercial use of documentation, images or other intellectual property is subject to the approval of Canadian Pacific Railway and requires a prior written agreement.

> To obtain research services or license reproductions, please send a detailed request to:

Canadian Pacific Archives
P.O. Box 6042 Station Centre-ville
Montreal, QC H3C 3E4
Telephone (514) 395-5135
Fax (514) 395-5132
e-mail: archives@cpr.ca

Note: *Unfortunately, employee records are not held by CP Archives and are not available for research purposes.*

Once upon a time

In the last decades of the twentieth century, Canadian Pacific Archives were in Windsor Station, Montreal, and the Archives were open to all employees of Canadian Pacific and to members of the public by appointment. In this century, researchers should check the current CP web page, verify the address and numbers given above and, if you have a specific question that you can set out clearly and simply, request help.

The CP Archives probably still holds their important collection of Canadian Pacific Publications. An employees magazine, *Passenger Traffic Bulletins* was published from August 1909 to June 1932, then *Staff Bulletin*, *Spanner*, and subsequently separate newspapers for the Rail and Hotel groups. These have been indexed to enable historians to locate major articles.

> **... The notable exception to this is that I have deliberately excluded the long lists of retirements, appointments, transfers, as well as the many recipes and other similar articles that would be considered of a personal nature. ...**
> –Stephen Lyons, Archivist. [authors' emphasis]

What this means is that if you know some CPR *historical* event that U.R. may have had a part in, the Archives might be able to help. Otherwise — what can we say?

Where Did the Microfilm Go?

Canadian Pacific kept detailed employee records for the people who worked for the company, even for quite short periods of time, from the late nineteenth century to the present time. These files were "stripped" when the person had not worked for the company for a length of time, or when pension benefits ceased, but the surviving records still provide a valuable summary of an individual's employment history with Canadian Pacific.

Gary Schroder of the Quebec Family History Society generously supplied this information on the CPR personnel records. Many years ago he was able to obtain a copy of the "employee card" giving a summary of his great grandfather's employment from 1884 to 1927. For many years John Flynn (1867–1927) was Chief Clerk in the Auditor of Freight and Telegraph Receipts office in Montreal. The card is stamped "DOCUMENTS DESTROYED October 15, 1937," which means the original sheets documenting his employment (letters of reference, notices of promotion etc.) were destroyed ten years after his death, but the card, or its photograph, probably still exists somewhere.

The staff records were microfilmed, probably in the 1950s, but in the early 1980s they were transferred from microfilm to microfiche to conserve space and simplify searches. The fate of the microfilms is not known.

Personnel records are not open to researchers; they are held by the Pensions and Benefits department at company headquarters, which moved from Montreal to Calgary in September 1996. Ten years ago, when I wrote asking if the records still existed, I received the following form letter:

> Dear Sir/Madam,
>
> This refers to your request for information concerning a former employee of this Company.
>
> In light of the current difficult competitive environment, we have had to make some significant cost reductions and as a result we no longer have the resources needed to research historical employee data. Accordingly I regret that we are unable to assist you in this matter.
>
> Sincerely (etc.)

All researchers recognize that privacy laws bar them from seeing any data on people now living, and we all know the time historical research requires. The CPR's inability to offer such costly service is understandable, particularly in the light of the ever-growing demands by family historians and genealogists. It would be nice to know, however, what historical employee data still exists? Was the microfilm destroyed? Has the Company considered depositing such historical data in some publicly accessible repository, be it archive, museum, library or historical association? They can place a twenty, or thirty or fifty year retention on it if confidentiality is a worry.

Some CPR Records You Can Access

These records were located through the Internet using Archives Canada (formerly CAIN - Canadian Archival Information Network), and searching under "Title" (on the pull-down search menu) for "Canadian Pacific Railway Fonds." It brought 33 hits, including:

Carleton County [New Brunswick] Historical Society which holds local CPR staff registers and payroll books;

City of Vancouver Archives have some CPR staff registers (1880–1914) and photographs (ca. 1912–193-).

Medicine Hat Museum and Art Gallery has a small CPR collection that includes ledgers of trainmen's earnings (1944) and trainmen's wage tickets (1938–1950), as well as documents of the Ladies Auxiliary to the Brotherhood of Railway Trainmen, 1900–1968, including a list of original members (1900).

Revelstoke Railway Museum whose holdings of the CPR Revelstoke Division's papers include crew reports, seniority lists, payroll and expenditure ledgers, timesheets, and personnel files. This collection also includes the Dick Farrell fonds, Karl Aho fonds, and those of other CPR employees.

Note that these finds are at a considerable distance from Head Office. In our early searches for personnel material, I had the distinct impression that the further U.R. worked from Headquarters, the better chance there was that records might escape the attention of Head Office Record Managers.

City Directories

In large western cities where the CPR was an important employer, early city directories are well worth searching. The most notable is *Henderson's Gazeteer and Directory of British Columbia, N.W.T., Manitoba, and North West Ontario* which in 1889 and 1890 has a separate "C.P.R. Pacific Division Directory" (1889: pp. 254–271) and "C.P.R. Western Division Directory" (1889: pp. 770–784) that list every CPR employee for these Divisions, their occupation and where stationed. Included in these volumes is a "City of Winnipeg Directory" that lists all employees of the "C.P.R. General Office" on Main Street. Earlier individual city directories also seem to have acquired employee lists from the CPR, for example in the 1884 and 1885 Directories of Winnipeg, the street entry for 761 Main Street (the CPR General Offices) fills seven to ten pages and lists every employee from the President down to the lowest car cleaner. By 1897 the listing was shorter but even in 1911 the "Canadian Pacific Railway" (alphabetical listing) included all officials' names, from Chief Clerks on up. In Montreal where the Head Offices were located, in 1894–95 both the CPR and GTR listings included all officials and agents, but for smaller eastern cities (and in smaller directories) there is almost nothing. It has already been noted that directory entries for individuals often indicate their job and who they work for.

Other Railway Company Archives

In 1967, as we celebrated the centennial of Confederation, a number of private companies decided to set up their own archives to preserve their history, but with the exception of the CNR and the CPR, only one other railway set up a formal archive. Alas, it was short-lived.

Ontario Northland Transportation Commission Archives

This Commission was established in 1946 to replace the Temiskaming and Northern Ontario Railway Commission. An Ontario Government Agency, it had its own archive in North Bay, Ontario, until it was closed in 1994. The archive's holdings, which are of considerable interest, do not appear to have been moved to the Archives of Ontario, which only lists Commission minute books in RG 14-39, and their whereabouts is unknown. The records are governed by the Ontario "Freedom of Information Protection of Privacy Act" that restricts information accessible to that on employees who have been dead for thirty years. The collection once included:

Employee Service Record Cards 1905–1986 cards list name, birth date, details of jobs

Seniority Lists for unionized employees (various dates) names in order of seniority - give date of entering service

The Quarterly 1946–1965 and **The Chevron** 1972–post 1993, the Company's newsletters existed and once could be consulted in the Reading Room. A number of the photographs in the collection are identified.

Albert Tucker (1923–), author of Steam into Wilderness, a history of the Ontario Northland, has deposited 9 audio cassettes at the Archives of Ontario that hold 24 oral history interviews. These are listed on the former CAIN, now Archives Canada Web site, CAIN No. 89731.

Via Rail

A Crown Corporation with headquarters in Montreal, founded in 1977; expect little access until 2007. Records should eventually be deposited at LAC.

Algoma Central Railway

The Sault Ste. Marie Public Library Archives has a large collection of records relating to industrial development, including the Algoma Central Railway Company. Their "virtual exhibit" on *Early Industrial Development in Sault Ste. Marie* is described at Archives Canada <www.archivescanada.ca>.

Other Railway Companies

Smaller railway lines probably preserve some records if only for their own use. However, in the past twenty years, small "branch lines" have been privatized, then bought, sold, traded or absorbed, to a point where it is almost impossible to keep track of them. Today's correct information will be totally wrong a year from now. If you can trace the whereabouts of a particular line (try local libraries), they might respond to an enquiry if you make it brief and to the point. They may even have deposited their records in a local archive.

Provincial and Other Archives

Every provincial archive holds some Government records relating to the building of railways within its territories, and may include microfilms of LAC holdings. The collected manuscripts of politicians and contractors often discuss proposed railway development, but rarely mention any but the most exalted railway people, and are of little genealogical interest.

The inventories of any repository's collection will almost certainly include railway-related documents of interest to some family historian; probably among a railway employee's or collector's private papers, in files of newspaper cuttings or a photography collections. Much ephemera survives: printed schedules of wages, rules and regulations, timetables and brochures. They name few names, but are of sociological interest. Watch for printed Seniority Lists of employees and for diaries of workers.

As well, when you know where U.R. worked, be sure to consult the regional Division of the Canadian Railroad Historical Association (CRHA), ask especially about photographs, timetables, Division Seniority Lists, and whether there are any taped oral histories. You might even join CRHA and collect your own copies of *Canadian Rail*. Remember that you can now consult the inventories of many repositories on the Internet at <www.archivescanada.ca>.

The following list is a representative sample only. It is intended to suggest the variety of record repositories and the types of records that you can find all across Canada.

Newfoundland

Records of the Newfoundland Railway are with those of the CNR at LAC, Ottawa. The Provincial Archives and Memorial University list few railway-related items in their Manuscript collections.

Prince Edward Island

Surviving records of the P.E.I. Railway are among those of the CNR (RG30) or RG 43 at the LAC. However, the Prince Edward Island Archives and Record Office has a collection of historical photographs, and its "virtual exhibit," Along the Line: Photographs of the PEI Railway can be found at the Archives Canada Web site <www.archivescanada. ca>. As well, the PEI Archives holds:

Accession 3639 (Pat McQuaid), photocopies of two Seniority Lists, Train Despatchers, Telegraphers etc. 1 Jan. 1941 & 31 Dec. 1958.

Accession 4211 (Muncy family Collection) includes the journal of the telegraph operator at Cape Traverse 1894–96.

Accession 4053, Harold Gaudet *Remembering Railroading on Prince Edward Island* (published by author, 1989).

Public Archives of Nova Scotia

RG 28 Government records relating to railways in Nova Scotia. The Finding Aid gives a brief history of each line and has good Contents Reports for most files.

Section 1, (e) Payrolls 1889

Section 2, Pay List 1854

Section 4, Vol.23, Payroll July 1899–summer 1900

Vols. 67 & 68, Pay Sheets, July–Aug. 1888

For new accessions see: Card Index under Miscellaneous - Railways: RG 28 "I.C.R. Insurance Association," 1 reel microfilm.

This appears to be a ledger used by a "Local Secretary" (Pictou Co., Nova Scotia) of the ICR Employees' R. [recreation?] and Insurance Association to record membership applications and certificates received & delivered. cf. LAC RG30, Accession 92–93/215.

MG 1, Vol.2470, Hunter Papers

[George Alexander Hunter, a CNR Conductor, retired 1946] clippings and notes on railway history. File no.14 "Memoranda and History Notes," includes data on accidents; File no.18 "Combined seniority list of Conductors, Halifax and Saint John District" lists Conductors, Brakemen & Trainmen from 1875 to 1914.

The Scotian Railway Society Collection is located at the PANS. This collection (mostly printed material) is typical of Railway Historical Society collections, covering railways across the continent, with good runs of trade papers and magazines. Typically, there are only a few personnel-related documents that someone saved and donated.

RG 28, Series "S"

Vol.4 (40,41,42) Notes on oral histories

Vol.22 (1,3,7) Payrolls, 1858–1859

Vol.41 (6) CNR List of seniority of employees 1931

Vol.50 (27) CNR Payroll, Brookfield, 1956

Vols.51 & 52 contain varied records from Brookfield 1953–1959

Vol.61 (1) - ICR, Red Pine Station Register, 1 Mar.–27 Sept.1909, Conductor of each train usually named.

Vol.61 (2) "Biographical Sketches of employees c. 1900": actually an unindexed ICR Staff ledger, probably Truro Division, entries to 1911. cf.LAC RG30, Accession 92–93/215.

Provincial Archives of New Brunswick,

RS 22 holds many Government records for early New Brunswick Railways; the "Subject Index" lists these and other RS holdings. There are no personnel records but a few payrolls survive for the New Brunswick Coal and Railroad Co. 1901–1913.

The New Brunswick Museum
277 Douglas Ave
Saint John, NB E2K 1E5
Railway-related papers in some 25 collections include ephemera and a few diaries of railway employees.

Moncton Museum
20 Mountain Road
Moncton, NB E1C 2J8
Collections relate to the history of Moncton and include some genealogical records, directories and railway ephemera.

Mount Allison University
Ralph Picard Bell Library
Sackville, NB E0A 3C0
European and North American Railway Pay Lists, May 1858 (Shediac/Moncton District).

Archives nationales du Québec
A guide to the holdings is available on microfiche and through their Internet Web site. Each of the nine regional branches has its own collection of the papers of local individuals and private companies.

Canadian Railway Historical Association Archives
Mail: P.O. Box 148
St. Constant, QC J5A 2G2
Their archives are located at:

Canadian Railway Museum at Delson/St. Constant
120 St. Pierre Street
St. Constant, QC J5A 2G9
tel: (514) 632-2410

Archives open by appointment. Office and archives may be contacted during business hours on week days. The collection includes documents, artifacts, ephemera and many photographs, as well as a large library, and the archive of *Canadian Rail*, however there is very little material relating to individuals or personnel. The holdings include a complete run of *Canadian Railway and Marine World* from 1898–1960. You may find valuable resources in the collection of any of the various railway histori-cal groups. (See Appendix C for addresses.)

Archives of Ontario

A Guide to the Holdings of the Archives of Ontario (1985), Microfiche. Index on final fiche. While index entry under "Railroads" seems to indicate material on many lines, examination shows most Railway-related documents are the private papers of individuals, promoters or engineers/builders. Typical is the Francis Shanly fonds, a description of which is found at <www.archivescanada.ca>, CAIN number 90610. A civil engineer, Francis Shanley (1820–1882) was associated with a great many lines, large and small. The following fonds, taken from the microfiche *Guide* should also come up in an online search: # 426 - Bailey, John C. (1872–1902); # 542 (MU 534) - Cheesworth, John W., Railroad builder (1901–1910!; # 1602 - Sims, Henry Augustus, papers (1855–1895); # 1626 - Steacy, Benjamin, records (1863–1887); #1647 - Swanson, Swan, papers (1897–1912) etc.

These entries may hold material of interest to family historians:

1580 Servais, Joseph, Autobiography (1864–1958), CNR references

1003 Heels, Charles H. Photographs of CNR trains, stations, bridges, etc.

1112 Kingsford, William, papers, includes scrapbooks related to Railways. (MU 1628 - 1663)

0789 Craig Diary, 1 Feb.–25 July 1911 (MS 352). Diary of a railway construction worker

0539 Chard, C.S., reminiscences (1906–1915), a station agent in Western Canada (MU 531)

1520 Railway Collection 1860–1949, 1'10" (MU 2369-2374, 3685)

Contains various printed ephemera, typescripts, notebooks, photo-graphs: Grand Trunk; Toronto, Hamilton and Buffalo; Toronto Nipiss-ing North Pacific Junction.

RG 14 Ministry of Transport and Communication (30 year restriction). Finding Aid for historical material only.

Hamilton Public Library, Hamilton,

Great Western Railway Co. of Canada, 1845–1882 (dates vary). Pay lists, time sheets, engine driver returns, casualty reports

Stratford and Perth Co. Archives, Stratford

Group photographs of CNR Shops Apprentices from the 1920s (also in LAC Photo Collection). Look for other GTR/CNR Shops-related material among private papers and manuscripts.

Trent University Archives, Peterborough

Grand Trunk Railway 1866–1874, Engineer Department, foreman's wage and material book.

University of Western Ontario Library, London

Grand Trunk Railway:

1903–1919, Time and Wage books, Yard staff

1898 Register of train departures and arrivals

1890–1894, 45 cm. Casualty Reports (London Division)

Provincial Archives of Manitoba and Saskatchewan Archives Board

Holdings generally relate to railway promotion or construction. Look for railway personnel-related material in Manuscript collections in university, city and community libraries, railway historical groups and museums.

Transcona Historical Museum

141 Regent Ave. West

Winnipeg, MB R2C 1R1

Tel: 204-222-0423; 204-222-0208

e-mail: transcona@istar.ca

The museum archives collects records of the Canadian National and Grand Trunk Pacific railways in all media, as well as records relating to Transcona itself. There were large shops here, so look for seniority lists, photographs, ephemera and oral histories.

Provincial Archives of Alberta

Northern Alberta Railways (pre-1 July 1929), cf. LAC, RG 30 IV H.

United Transportation Union, records, CNR Western Regions, see also at LAC, MG 28, I 216.

Glenbow Museum Archives

130 - 9th Ave., S.E.

Calgary, AB T2G 0P3

403-268-4100

Glenbow Archives A Guide to the Holdings, comp. & ed. Susan M.
    Kooyman and Bonnie Woelk, 2 vols. (Calgary, 1992).
Brotherhood of Locomotive Firemen and Enginemen, Sandstone City
    Lodge No. 635, 1903–1968, 37.5 cm. Inventory available.
  Minute Books, 1903–35; convention delegates 1931, 1968;
    Membership lists 1967.
Brotherhood of Railway Carmen of America.
  Kitchin Lodge No. 145, 1914–1934, 37.5 cm. - Minutes etc.
  Ladysmith Lodge No. 42, 1911–1936 - Minutes, 1911–1917; dues
    receipt books 1933–36.
United Transportation Union, CPR Western Region, 1892–1984, Minutes
    and Correspondence; also microfilm of related papers.

Note: Glenbow Archives have a large collection of newspapers on microfilm from towns and cities in all the Prairie provinces. Holdings also include CPR land settlements records, oral history material and an important collection of photographs.

Provincial Archives of British Columbia

Pacific Great Eastern Railway [predecessor of BC Railway Co.]
Add. MSS 106, 1911–1929, 15 vols., detailed file list includes:
Construction expense accounts, 1918–1922
Payrolls Victoria Office, 1921–1925
Add. MSS 483, 1920–1934, correspondence and Seniority Lists,
    Brotherhood of Locomotive Engineers.
Sound and Moving Image Division: check for taped interviews and
    transcripts that Robert D. Turner used for *Railroaders* (1981).

Kamloops Museum, Kamloops

CPR Kamloops Section,
1890 and 1927, Journal of workers based in Kamloops
Brotherhood of Railroad Trainmen, Kamloops Lodge, 1895–1954
    Ledgers, Record Books, attendance records (years vary).

Yukon Archives

The White Pass and Yukon Railway Co., an English holding company, ran four local companies: British Yukon Railway Co.; British Columbia Yukon Railway Co.; British Navigation Co., and Pacific and Arctic

Railway and Navigation Co. In 1951 these became the White Pass and Yukon Corp. Ltd. "Records of the White Pass and Yukon Routes" include entire corporate organization. Railway related are:

1942–1955 Daily Time Returns and Delay Reports of Engine and Train Employees

1944 Monthly Time Books for Railway Section Crews.

A large collection of photographs pertaining to company operations, both construction and operation exist. There are also records of people seeking employment on the company's riverboats. If U.R. worked in the Yukon, you will find the Archives most helpful.

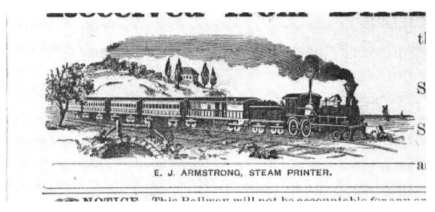

E. J. ARMSTRONG, STEAM PRINTER.

This image of a steam train was taken from an Intercolonial Railway Traffic Department shipping form dated June 15, 1888.

Six

Wrecks and Their Whereabouts

Records Are Hard to Find

Almost every family with railway connections has a "wreck" story, and most want to find out more about the event. In the first century of railways, accidents, injuries and deaths were common, so common in fact that railway workers had a difficult time obtaining insurance. In the various Canadian railway archives you would think we might find files labelled "wrecks" or "fatalities." Alas, although there are some, they are few and far between.

Carl Vincent, a senior archivist at the then National Archives of Canada, dealt for years with every aspect of the Canadian railway records in the Government Archives Division. When asked about material on wrecks or deaths, he said he had never seen anything in RG 30. He suggested any records that were kept were probably in the Legal Department and their files were not in RG 30 but still with the company.

Since then, however, some Headquarters, and some Legal Records (Western and Central Regions) have been accessioned, and contain a few files on claims for personal injuries or deaths, see Chapter Four, RG 30 V-A-9 g & h, and new accessions, item 3, MIKAN No. 49220 "Miscellaneous Records 1839–1982." The Finding Aid, 30-18, searchable on ArchiviaNet, is alphabetical so right away you find a smattering of "Accidents—collisions," "Accidents—derailments," then "— general," "— level crossings," "— misc.," in the list of 3,815 items. Nevertheless, information on accidents and deaths is not complete and is difficult to find outside of newspapers.

That's Not Possible

Whenever you tell this to former railroad employees they say "That's not possible! We all had to fill out long reports every time a cow got pushed off the track, much less someone getting killed or equipment damaged." "We had to survey the site of any accident, check the sight lines and everything else for the report." "There were annual reports every railroad company had to file with the Government listing every fatality. There must be records—lots of them!"

We agreed. So, when we saw in *Canadian Rail* #461 (Nov.–Dec. 1997) that Hugh A. Halliday had just published *WRECK! Canada's Worst Railway Accidents*, we hoped he would provide details about his sources. The book describes, with maps and pictures, thirty major railway wrecks, from 1854 to 1986. If your wreck is among the thirty, here is your information. About his sources he says: "Much was gleaned from newspaper accounts of accidents and of the coroner's inquests that followed them." Halliday also credits "reports by the Board of Transport Commissioners on investigations of accidents in the 1940s and 1950s."

Since Carl Vincent compiled *RG 46 Records of the Canadian Transport Commission* (1984) in the General Inventory Series, he knew that their Central Registry files, 1904–1973, did include "fatal accidents to individuals," but also knew most RG 46 files are very difficult to access. That may explain why Halliday's footnotes state he found the Board's reports at the National Archives, but in RG 12 (which is Department of Transport), Vol. 610. The ArchiviaNet index to Government Records, for RG 12, Vol. 610, brings up seven files. Five have the keywords "accidents - collisions and derailments" and include wrecks at Almonte, Ontario; Dugald, Manitoba, and Canoe River, British Columbia, which are included in *Wrecks!*, plus a derailment at Waterville, Quebec, and a wreck at St. Cyrville, Quebec. The other two files are "Accounting and Finance"—alphabetical arrangement again? Did Halliday select these wrecks for his book because they were the only ones easy to document? Or are they in the ArchiviaNet index because he dug them out for his book?

Start with Newspapers

Halliday relied primarily on newspapers, and this is where any accident research starts. Most editors considered railway accidents news and reported anything local. According to Glenn Wright, in the 1930s the editor of the *Calgary Eye-Opener* hated the CPR, and reported every CPR wreck, usually with a photograph. On the other hand, because of security considerations, wrecks that occurred in wartime probably will not be reported in the newspapers.

Newspapers, however, are the source of most published accounts. *Canadian Rail* carries occasional stories of notable wrecks. Fred F. Angus's twelve-page article about "The Penny Wreck Centennial, 1897–1997" in No. 456 (Jan.–Feb. 1997), quotes extensively from newspaper reports of both the wreck and the official investigations, but cites no Government records. The wreck, in which two passengers were killed, a cabinet minister and several prominent people injured, and six tons of newly minted copper one-cents coins spread across the ice of Palmer's Pond near Dorchester, New Brunswick, was widely reported and became a local legend.

John Thompson's story of the wreck of an immigrant train at Beloeil, Quebec, "The Immigrant Special, June 29, 1864" in *Canadian Rail* No. 471, relies almost entirely on newspaper accounts with only one official document, a Grand Trunk Railway "Return of the Accidents and Casualties that have occurred … during the half year ending 30 June, 1864. Made in compliance with provisions of the 'Accidents on Railways Act', 20 Victoria, Chapter 12th, Section 14." So we know that as early as 1857, all accidents did have to be reported, but this printed form contains about two lines of information.

Researching My Wreck

To explain what records exist for more contemporary accidents Althea decided to research a known wreck. My family's "wreck story" was the Circus Train, or why we were given free passes when the circus came to town. I was too young to remember the event, but heard the story many times. My father was General Superintendent Car Equipment for the Atlantic Region of the CNR in Moncton. One summer weekend he and some railway friends went fishing at Kent Junction where they had a camp. You could see the cabin from the main CNR line and it was pointed out to me on many trips. "That's where your father was when the circus train was wrecked. We were at the cottage and they sent someone from Moncton to find him. Hunted all over Moncton for the others too, and there they were at the wreck within the hour."

One detail fixed itself in my young mind. Some of the roustabouts had slung their hammocks under the cars, and when the train was derailed, men were crushed under the big beams that supported the wooden cars. Normally nothing could be done until the wrecking train with its big cranes arrived. My father told me how the circus people took bales of hay, built a ramp (or was it steps) so the elephants could leave their cars. Then, trainers had an elephant take each end of the beam and lift so the men could be freed.

Date? Place? Newspapers.

When exactly did it happen? Sometime before 1932 when we moved to Toronto. There must be newspaper stories about a circus train that was wrecked north of Moncton, and I once saw a story in a magazine, probably *The Atlantic Advocate*. As luck would have it, I had kept that story, but it could have been found by consulting Periodical Indexes (Canadian in this case) and then securing a copy of the article through interlibrary loan. *The Oxford Guide to Library Research* explains many such sources. Better yet, ask your local reference librarians for help, they will know about both published and online indexes to both newspapers and periodicals.

The story was by C.L. Woods, whose memories were recounted in the June, 1979 issue of *The Atlantic Advocate* and illustrated by banner headlines from Moncton's *The Daily Times* of Monday, July 21 1930 announcing "FOUR DEAD IN CIRCUS TRAIN WRECK." The fledgling reporter had a photographer with him so there was a picture of the wrecked Al G. Barnes Circus train at Canaan Station on the morning of Sunday, July 20, 1930.

So we know it happened at Canaan Station, at 6:55 a.m. when nine cars jumped the rails, including sleeping and equipment cars. The Station Agent would have known that CNR executives were a few miles up the line at their fishing camp and probably sent a hand-car for them. Then it would be their responsibility to handle things. They would have been on site before any emergency wreck train could be made up and get there from Moncton, though both wrecking crews and a hospital train with volunteer doctors and nurses arrived soon.

This was big enough news that it would have been reported in other newspapers, and there could well be interviews in the Moncton and Saint John papers with both circus employees and the railway people. Eventually there would be a coroner's inquest to be reported and there might be other pictures that were published. If I wanted to know fuller details about the wreck, newspapers would be the easiest source to access. However, newspaper reports can contain errors and interviews are sometimes garbled. What I hoped to find was official information from railway reports.

Given the date, time and place, of a wreck on the CNR main line, in which four people were killed, what can be found in official Government Records? What about Halliday's "reports by the Board of Transport Commissioners"? He found them in RG12 (Department of Transport), but the Board of Transport Commissioners is RG 46. Both are Government of Canada records and the Archives makes available a variety of guides to Government Records both published and on the Internet. When you are searching them it is most important to read their brief outlines of "Administrative History" that show how agencies or boards changed both their names and functions over the years. Note the dates when changes occur.

Department of Transport—RG 12

Established in 1936 by the amalgamation of the Departments of Marine (RG 42) and Railways and Canals (RG 43) plus the Civil Aviation Branch of the Department of National Defence (RG 25), among the Department of Transport's responsibilities is the safety of all forms of transportation. A search in ArchiviaNet, limited to RG 12 and keywords "railways - collision" brought up an April 1873 claim for personal injury to John Black in a collision on the ICR. Other keywords like "derailment" and "fatal accident" were equally unproductive, with only one other claim, by E.A. Jones. Both claims files were in Vol. 1848. RG 12 vol. 610 and its five wrecks are noted above, but I found them only by knowing and using the volume number.

Canadian Transport Commission—RG 46

In RG 46 the earliest holdings are Records of the Board of Railway Commissioners of the United Provinces of Canada (1857–) that, at Confederation, became the Railway Committee of the Privy Council, then in 1904 the Board of Railway Commissioners again. In 1938 it absorbed two other boards (Air and Maritime) and was renamed Board of Transport Commissioners. Finally, in 1967 it became the Canadian Transport Commission.

For a wreck in 1930, I should look for records of the Board of Railway Commissioners. However, in ArchiviaNet, records of earlier Boards are found under their current title: RG 46 Canadian Transport Commission. In searching the Government Records Index using Detailed Search, entering 46 [not RG 46] in the slot for Record Group Number, and using Keywords: railway accident, I got 156 hits, largely from the first quarter of the twentieth century, but a couple in the 1940s. To limit entries to "my wreck" I added New Brunswick to the Keywords. That produced four files in Series C-II-1 from the years 1912–1915, none on the ICR. Two were CPR, and while the file titles spell out Canadian Pacific Railway, "CPR" does work as a Keyword. Place names and abbreviations for provinces (like NB) are also useful keywords. Each reference a search produces will have a Volume number and a File number, so if *your wreck* does appear, you can secure the complete dossier, requesting it by the RG number, i.e. 46; plus BOTH the Volume (box) number, and the File number. A File number alone is not much help, though there exist some printed sources for finding these numbers as I discovered.

RG 46, Series C-II-1

Series C is the records of the Board of Railway Commissioners, 1904–1938, and Board of Transport Commissioners, 1938–1967. C-II-1 is the Central Registry Files, 1904–1973 (Vols. 489–523, 1337–1589; with further accessions received after 1984 through 2001) that, according to the 1984 General Inventory. "cover all aspects of the Board's activities. Among the more frequently encountered subjects are the establishment and removal of railway stations, fatal accidents…," as well as abandonment of lines, fares, tariffs and various rates.

In the Central Registry, all the correspondence, reports, memoranda and orders related to a single subject (e.g. investigation of a fatal accident) were gathered together in one file that was given a number by which it could be located. However, these "numbers were not allotted in a logical order, and files on closely related subjects (for example, accidents fatal to individuals) may appear in many different portions of the numerical system" (Vincent, 1984, p. 22). When I consulted the detailed finding aid, FA 46-21, this proved only too true.

FA 46-21 fills two 4" (10 cm) Hollinger boxes, each with four folders, each folder holding about 2.5 cm. of accordion folded computer print-out that are "box lists." These itemize the contents of each volume (box)—there are at least 313—listing the file titles with some dates, and file number. As I scanned the box lists I realized the files were not boxed in numerical order, nor chronologically, nor by related subjects. Clearly the file numbers were not allocated in any logical order, and were assigned volumes (that is, boxed) in random order, possibly based on when they were accessioned, or perhaps when the accessions were processed.

There is a printed list in each FA 46-21 folder listing which accessions are in what volumes, but all that tells is the dates of the accessions, largely in the computer era, 1981–82, 1985–86, and more throughout the 1990s. So the data is in a computer somewhere, and I am assured is scheduled to be added to ArchiviaNet, so eventually it may turn up in a useable form.

Sessional Papers and Departmental Reports

Where else to look? Would a report of the Board of Railway Commissioners be printed in *Sessional Papers* or *Departmental Reports*? For some years they are, but not for others. I was lucky; 1930 is the last year *Departmental Reports* are on the open shelves of the Library Reading Room and while most *Departmental Reports* end in March 1930, the Railway Commissioners' covers the entire year.

The Report is primarily concerned with statistical records and year-to-year comparisons of totals of various types of accidents and the increase or decrease of accidents and fatalities (2,427 accidents were reported in 1930). However, in Appendix C there were lists of each accident the Board investigated, sorted by type. The circus train was a derailment and in this list there it was one line, telling me what I already knew, but giving the file number [File] "22874/July 20/C.N.R./Canaan, N.B./killed 4/injured 19."

Back to FA 46-21 with a File number (22874), where lack of time and the almost completely random order of files in volumes (boxes) defeated me. A long and systematic search of the printed box-lists, or access to the database and software (if it is not obsolete) might have produced a Vol. (box) number.

There must be a wealth of material about countless wrecks in RG 46 C-II-1, but it is almost completely inaccessible until the database used for the box-list is added to ArchiviaNet. So far, only a few wrecks have made it.

The Board's published Reports, 1904 through 1930, may occasionally be helpful. There were complete lists of each type of accident, including pages of "highway crossing accidents" in 1930, but in 1913 only lists of collisions and derailments that gave file numbers (Paper 20c, pp. 423–427). In 1909 (Paper 20c, pp. 200 & ff.) listed "Causes of One Hundred and Twenty-two Prominent Train Accidents Investigated and Reported by the Board," but a random check of other years failed to turn up any such reports by the Board of Railway Commissioners.

Try Other Reports and Sources

In the Report of the Railway and Canal Department in 1909 (*SP*, No. 20, part II, pp. 138–143) I found the Intercolonial Railway's Statement of Casualties for the Year Ended March 31, 1908. That tabulation gave the date, time of day, train number, train description (passenger, express, yard engine etc.), name of the Conductor, Driver, engine number, place, person injured, whether they were a passenger or employee or neither, the particulars of the accident, extent of injuries and verdict. It was fascinating reading, but I failed to find similar lists in other years I sampled.

Wrecks in R231 Accessions

A couple of recent accessions in RG 30/R231 do include some data: see Chapter Four.

MIKAN 47523 - (vol. 14434) [access 10] accidents and collisions 1950–1977;

MIKAN 136006 - Agreements of The Grand trunk Railway Company of Canada 1859–1930 FA 30-106 (paper) lists "semi-annual returns of GTR accident and casualty lists, June 1858–Dec. 1864" which include number and description of train, date, time of day, place of accident, name(s) of person(s) killed.

Royal Canadian Mounted Police - RG 18

The Genealogy Desk's railway ring binder also reminds us to look at the Annual Reports of the Northwest Mounted Police, or after 1920 the Royal Canadian Mounted Police (RCMP). This force was responsible for recording deaths in the Territories, but their *Sessional Paper/Annual Reports* commonly list the crimes, trials, and other misdoings in the various Departments. Each Department reports separately, so if you know of an accident in a given year at a known place, there might well be a reference to it. You might be able to use this information as a guide to finding fuller documentation in RG 18.

Another Early Source

Dominion Annual Register and Review (Montreal: Dawson Brothers, 1878–1886) includes annual obituary lists and a "Journal of Remarkable Occurrences" which includes accidental deaths and suicides, fires, trials, shipwrecks and railway accidents, listed chronologically. There is a Name index and a Subject index near the end of each volume.

Do Not Forget Art and Photo Records

Train wrecks were news. In early years, artists made drawings for periodicals. In the twentieth century, newspaper editors usually sent photographers with their reporters. Check the newspapers first, then check with the local library. Library and Archives Canada have a vast collection that almost certainly contains illustrative material, though finding it may be a challenge because of subject indexing.

To sum it up, your "family wreck" is probably recorded somewhere in Government records, but it can be with the CNR Legal Department, Department of Transport or Board of Railway Commissioners, and it will be hard to find. You are far more likely to find an account of your wreck in newspapers, or if you are unsure of the date, look through local and regional histories that may well include accounts of local tragedies.

Seven

Canadian Patents

No. 512 — WILLIAMS, (J.,) of the City of Montreal, for a "New and useful improvement in the blast of Locomotive Engines." Quebec, dated 20 April 1855.

No. 519 — BOWNAN, (W.,) [sic] of the City of Hamilton, for "A new and useful mode of constructing Railway Car Wheels." Quebec, dated 4 May, 1855.

No. 521 — BOWMAN, (W.,) [sic] of the City of Hamilton, for "A new and useful improvement in the construction of Railway Cars." Quebec, dated 12 January 1855.

No. 529 — McDOUGALL, (R.,) of the City of Toronto, in the County of York, for an "Improved Oil Box for oiling axles of Rail Car Wheels, Quebec, dated 8th June, 1855.

No. 532 — YOUNG, (J.R.,) BROWN, (R.S.,) DAVIS, (H.,) all in the city of Hamilton, for a "self-opening Railway Gate," Quebec, dated 14 June 1855.

Those patents are taken from two pages, covering a mere half-year, in a 222-page *List of Canadian Patents from the Beginning of the Patent Office, June 1824, to the 31st of August 1872* (Ottawa, 1979).

If U.R. Ancestor worked for a railway he probably had ideas about how to improve some mechanical detail of cars, engines, gates or switches. If he patented it and it became a part of your family lore, you may want to find more about the patent. Patents are almost all held by Library and Archives Canada, but—and it is a big *but*—you must know the Patent Number.

No one in the Archives could explain to me how to find the number, yet it proved quite simple once I discovered the published sources in the Library. Perhaps because a searchable Canadian Intellectual Property Office (CIPO) database is online (at http://cipo.gc.ca/) starting with patents issued in the early 1920s and running to almost the end of the twentieth century, people have forgotten about the printed sources.

Who Created the Records

Patent legislation in the colonies of Upper and Lower Canada was administered by the respective Provincial Secretary, but in 1852, after the union of the Canadas into a single colony, the responsibility was assigned to the Minister of Agriculture of the Province of Canada.

After Confederation the registration of patents, trademarks, copyright and industrial design remained with the Department of Agriculture until 1918. The Department of Trade and Commerce took it over until 1927 when it became the responsibility of the Secretary of State. In 1967 Consumer and Corporate Affairs assumed control of the administration of intellectual property.

RG 105

The patent records from 1861 to 1985, now with the Archives of Canada, are grouped together in Record Group RG 105, where the records are arranged in a sort of chronological order and consist of the following types of documents:

- industrial design registrations
- copyright registration and indexes
- trademark applications and indexes to registrations
- exemplifications of patents and inventions
- copies of Canadian and American radio patents
- registers of correspondence and letterbooks on copyright, trademarks and industrial design (Lovering, 1991, p. 120).

When dealing with RG 105 be sure to distinguish between patents of inventions (railway car-couplings, improvements on locomotive boilers, new improved corsets, etc.) and the registration of industrial designs (such as cast iron stoves or souvenir spoons), which are quite a separate set of records. Copyright registration of written and published material, as well as trademarks, are yet other protected categories, and all are in different Series.

The Patent Office organizes its records of granted patents by the Patent Number. Consecutive numbers are assigned as the patents are granted, and so they are in more or less chronological order, but if you only know the date, finding a specific patent is problematic. A first series covers those patents granted under various acts in Lower Canada, Upper Canada and the Province of Canada. A new series, starting again at 1, covers those granted under the Canadian Patent Act of 1869. This continues to the present day.

The Patent Office from time to time issued lists of patents granted, in numerical order. For most of the nineteenth century and up to 1969, these are indexed published records, many of which, particularly after 1873, describe and include a drawing of the inventions. All years from 1824 are indexed by the name of the patent holder, while most are also indexed by the type of invention.

Lists and Indexes

The easiest way to locate copies of the following printed lists and indexes is to use Library and Archives Canada's online AMICUS Union Catalogue, which will give the locations of copies in libraries across Canada. Because the titles can be confusing, the easy way to locate the titles in the catalogue is to use the Amicus numbers that are given below with each title.

Patents, 1824–1855

Patents of Canada, AMICUS No. 2171137, published in two volumes (Toronto: Lovell & Gibson, 1860–1865), is indexed, and covers patents issued before Confederation by the provinces of Upper and Lower Canada, vol. 1: 1824–1849; vol.2: 1849–1855. These are now "rare books" and LAC copies are not available for interlibrary loan. However, both volumes are available on microfiche:

Vol.1 1824–1849 AMICUS No. 6648550 CIHM/ICMH microfiche No. 49353

Vol.2 1849–1855 AMICUS No. 6648626 CIHM/ICMH microfiche No. 49354

Each volume starts with descriptions of the individual patents, in numerical sequence, complete with names(s) and address(es) of patentee(s). The index follows, listing both the patentee and type of invention, then such illustrations as have survived, again by number. Each volume fills 7 fiches and these are filmed in the same order as the original publication.

Patents, 1855–1872

After 1855 the official information on patent numbers, inventions and patentees is available in unindexed list form only. There exists a *List of Canadian Patents from the beginning of the patent office (June 1824), till the 1st of January 1869*. Published in Ottawa by the Times Steam Power Works in 1868, it has 156 pages, but no index. AMICUS No.: 9174472.

Much easier to obtain because it exists in facsimile will be *List of Canadian Patents, from the beginning of the Patent Office, June 1824, to the 31st of August, 1872*. AMICUS no.: 2385962. It was printed in Ottawa by Roger Maclean in 1882, but also by Gordon Publications and Reproductions (Ottawa, 1979). It fills 222 pages and is simply a list, giving number, name of patentee, address and what the invention is. Some railway "improvements" are quoted at the beginning of this chapter. There is no index in this facsimile of the "Blue Book," however Gordon G. Phillips, publisher of the facsimile, has prepared a separate index (see below). The Patents are listed in two series.

- Series 1: patents that were granted under the various acts in Lower Canada, Upper Canada and the Province of Canada.

- Series 2 covers patents granted after Confederation (1 July 1867) under the Patent Act of 1869. There is some overlap of dates because patents applied for under the pre–1869 acts were granted under them.

In the *Index of Inventors and Inventions for Canadian Patents 1824 to 1872* (Ottawa: 1983), AMICUS No. 4737604, G.G. Phillips indexes the first Series by Inventor, Invention and Residence of Inventor, but for the second Series there is *no index of inventions*. In other words, between 1869 and 1872, you can easily find U.R.'s patents, because you know his name, but hunting for patents on "Railway car-coupling" or "improved boilers" the researcher must read through 1,644 entries in very small print.

Patents after 1872

After 1872 things get much better. From 1873–1875, G.E. Desbarats of Montreal issued the *Canadian Patent Office Record and Mechanics' Magazine*; in 1876 the title was changed to the *Canadian Mechanics' Magazine and Patent Office Record* (Ottawa: Burland-Desbarats Litho Co., 1876–1878 [v.4, no.1 (Jan.1876)–v.6, no.12 (Dec. 1878)] and then became the *Scientific Canadian Mechanics' Magazine and Patent Office Record* (Montreal: Burland-Desbarats Lith. Co. [1879–1882]. This was followed by *The Canadian Magazine of Science and the Industrial Arts, Patent Office Record* ([Montreal?]: 1883–1891?).

These slim little magazines were issued each month as two separate entities. Each issue of each magazine has its own index, but for some years there were also annual indexes of the patents. In the eighteenth and nineteenth centuries, subscribers to such magazines often had their copies bound in annual volumes. The arrangement and placement of indexes and illustrations might vary with the taste of the owner or the whim of the bookbinder.

The National Library run of the serials are sometimes bound annually, but in two parts: 12 issues of the *Mechanics Magazine* or *Scientific Canadian* or whatever, followed by 12 issues of *The Canadian Patent Office Record*. The 1882 volume is available in this form, but, as well, the *Patent Office Record* issues for 1882, 1883 and 1884 are bound together: first the three annual indexes, then the monthly patent descriptions, then the monthly drawings.

The Canadian Institute for Historical Microreproductions clearly found the arrangement of bound issues confusing. In the first issue, the *Canadian Patent Office Record and Mechanics Magazine* claimed to include all the patents issued, but in the fiches of the magazines one finds very few patents, nor is there is any list of grantees. CIHM-ICMH issued four (4) microfiche of the four magazines with titles that are correct, but misleading because they *do not include* the *Canadian Patent Office Record*:

p04862 *Canadian Patent Office Record and Mechanics' Magazine* (1873–1875; vols.1–3) AMICUS No. 9764039, which is *only* the *Mechanics' Magazine*.

p04864 *Canadian Mechanics' Magazine and Patent Office record* (1876–1878; vols. 4–6) AMICUS No. 9765059, again, *only* the *Magazine.*

p04865 *Scientific Canadian Mechanics' Magazine and Patent Office Record* (1879–1882; vols. 7–10) AMICUS No. 9766241, *only* the *Magazine.*

p04873 *Canadian Magazine of Science and the Industrial Arts, Patent Office Record* (1883–1891; vols. 11–19) AMICUS No. 9819756, *only* the *Magazine.*

Finding the Fifth Fiche

Because all the patent information is in a semi-separate publication or appendix, this was filmed separately. For patent information (index, text and drawing) you must secure a copy of: p04863 *The Canadian Patent Office Record.* The issues reproduced are Vol.1, no.1 (Mar. 1873) through vol.28, no.12 (Dec. 1900). Some texts are in French. *AMICUS no.: 9766135,*

The microfiche can be borrowed, and copied, but be very careful when using the AMICUS catalogue, either at the Library or for interlibrary loan, to get this exact title, because there are a number of variants. Use the AMICUS no.: 9766135, and as well, specify the CIHM No. p04863.

If you succeed in obtaining the great bundle of microfiche—and when I was doing my research I concluded this particular fiche was a focal point for Murphy's Law because everything that could possibly go wrong, did—the next game is to "Find the Index." Do not expect consistency.

Game: Find the Index

Patents are indexed by the name of the patentee and by the type of invention. Sometimes a monthly index is filmed with each issue, sometimes all the monthly indexes are filmed together at the end of the December issue (1891), sometimes a cumulative annual index is filmed before the January issue (1892). The indexing varies in quality, so if you do not find something you think should be there, check under "Improved," "New" and "Machine for...." The index entries give the patent number. In the cumulative indexes only the patent number is given with no indication of which monthly issue it is in, so the next game is to "Find the patent" in the text material, which is arranged in numerical order by patent number.

These entries give the full names of the patent holder/holders or assignees, city and state/province, the date the patent was issued and a description, in very small print, of why the invention is new and original. If it is a renewal of an earlier patent, that number is given. For most, there is also a small drawing, in a separate section with fifteen to a page, also arranged in numerical order.

Now Find the Drawing

"Find the drawing" is the last game. The filming of the drawings is also inconsistent, sometimes at the end of each issue, sometimes at the end of December. Those for the first fiches, March 1873 through March 1874 are at the end of March 1874, though a couple of pages are missing.

Patents after 1900

The *Canadian Patent Office Record and Register of Copyright and Trade Marks* continued to be printed, in Ottawa by the King's/Queen's printer, beginning with vol.20 (1892), ending with vol. 97, no.25 (June 1969). The Library and Archives of Canada hold 1892–93, 95, 97, and 1900–1960 & 1961–1969, but most are not available for Interlibrary Loan. AMICUS nos.: 1839164 and 805183.

The run from vol. 1, no.2 May 1873 to vol. 97, No. 25 (24 June 1969) has been microfilmed by Micromedia Ltd., Toronto, 1981. AMICUS No. 25546912 and Micromedia may also have issued it on microfiche, AMICUS No. 9306715, though title and dates covered are not clear in the catalogue entry.

CIPO Database

Remember that after about 1923 there is a searchable CIPO database on the Internet with full information on patents issued from the early 1920s to almost the end of the twentieth century (http://patents1.ic.gc.ca/intro-e.html). This database lets one search for, and look at some seventy-five years of Canadian patents, starting in about 1924 using an inventor's name or company name search, or type of invention. Remember that a railway employee might have had to assign any patent to the company employing him if such inventing was part of his job, and his name may or may not be included as an associate.

The Real Thing

If you must see the actual documents, those are held by the Library and Archives Canada in RG 105, but there are no indexes and box-list type finding aids are "not in the computer" as yet. That being the case, you *must know* the patent number, and with that—and luck—someone might be able to find the file for you over in Gatineau, but it may take considerable time for them to locate the box (Volume number) the file is in.

Appendix A

Abbreviations

A.A.R. Association of American Railroads (formerly A.R.A.)

AC&HB Algoma Central & Hudson Bay

ACR Algoma Central Railway

AFL American Federation of Labor

A.R.A. American Railway Association (now A.A.R.)

BCR British Columbia Railway (formerly PGER)

BLE Brotherhood of Locomotive Engineers

BLF Brotherhood of Locomotive Firemen

BLF&E Brotherhood of Locomotive Firemen & Enginemen

BRT Brotherhood of Railroad Trainmen

CBRTGW Canadian Brotherhood of Railway, Transport and General Workers

C & O Chesapeake & Ohio (Chessie)

CGW Chicago Great Western Railroad

CN Canadian National (formerly CNR - new logo 1961)

CNR Canadian National Railways (now CN)

CNoR Canadian Northern Railway

CP Canadian Pacific [Ltd.] (Company name after 1971)

CPR Canadian Pacific Railway (now CP or CPRail)

CRHA Canadian Railway Historical Association

CVR   Central Vermont Railway

DAR   Dominion Atlantic Railway

D&H   Delaware and Hudson Railway (bought by CPR 1991)

dist.   District

div.   Division

GN   Great Northern

GTWR   Grand Trunk Western Railroad (now CNR)

GTPR   Grand Trunk Pacific Railway (now CNR)

GWR   Great Western Railroad of Canada (now CNR)

ICR   Intercolonial Railway (now CNR)

ILO   International Labor Organization

jct.   junction

K&P   Kingston and Pembroke (Kick and Push)

LAC   Library and Archives Canada (former NA & NLC)

MC   Michigan Central

MeC   Maine Central

NA   National Archives of Canada (now LAC)

NJRy   Napierville Junction Railway

NP   Northern Pacific

NYC   New York Central

ONR   Ontario Northland Railway (formerly TNOR)

PAC   Public Archives of Canada (now LAC)

PANS   Provincial Archives of Nova Scotia

PEI [Ry]   Prince Edward Island [Railway]

PGER   Pacific Great Eastern Railway (now BCR)

PP&J   Pontiac & Pacific Junction (Push, Pull & Jerk)

RPO   Railway Post Office

sub./ subd.   Subdivision

TH&B   Toronto, Hamilton & Buffalo

UTU   United Transportation Unions

Appendix B

Canadian Railway Chronology

This chronology has been expanded from that in the first edition, particularly with regard to the twentieth century. Most events concern activities that might affect employees, or turn up in family scrapbooks or collections as ephemera. For a more detailed chronological history of Canadian Railways' expanding operations, 1900–1959, see Fred Angus's "Farewell to the Twentieth Century, Part 1," in *Canadian Rail*, No.479 (Nov.–Dec. 2000) and for the changes to service and equipment and closing of lines from 1960 to 1999, see "Farewell to the Twentieth Century Part 2," *Canadian Rail* No. 482 (May–June 2001). Donald MacKay's *The People's Railway* includes "A Brief Chronology" of CN from 1919 to 1992. Pierre Burton's two-volume history of the building of the CPR has very detailed chronologies through 1885.

1832 Champlain & Saint Lawrence Railway authorized by act of Lower Canada Legislature

1836, 21 July First train operated on Champlain & St. Lawrence

1839, May Steam locomotives for Pictou Railway arrive in Nova Scotia See *Canadian Rail* No. 474 (Jan.–Feb. 2000), p.13

1840 Albion Mine RR opened in Nova Scotia (6 miles)

1846, 9 June Enabling Act for Montreal & Lachine Rail Road

1846 At Quyon (Chats Falls) a horse-drawn railroad operated by the Union Forwarding and Railway Co. until about 1879

1847, 19 November First train on Montreal & Lachine Rail Road

1854 Carillon & Grenville Railway built (proposed in 1840)

1850, 10 August Charter for the Bytown & Prescott Railway (work starts 1851). Became Ottawa & Prescott Railway in 1855

1851 Construction begun on Great Western Railway (Toronto to Buffalo); completed Niagara Falls to Windsor, January 1855, and to Toronto December 1860.

1851 Charter for Montreal & Kingston Railroad (work starts 1852)

1851, 31 July Passage of law requiring that all railways to receive Government assistance were to be built to 5 ft. 6 in. gauge.

1852 Legislation setting up Grand Trunk Railway (line completed Montreal to Toronto in 1856)

1852 First mail carried on Canadian railway.

1853, 16 May First steam train in Upper Canada, Toronto to Aurora

1853, July Completion of Atlantic & St. Lawrence (Montreal to Portland), leased (999 years) by GTR

1854, 25 December First train on Bytown & Prescott Railway

1855 Northern Railway, completed to Collingwood

1854 to 1858 Nova Scotia Railway built, Halifax-Truro-Windsor; extended to Pictou in 1867

1857, 12 March Desjardin Canal railway disaster (near Hamilton)

28 May "Accidents on Railways Act" passed to increase railway safety.

1857 First sleeping car (anywhere) built in Hamilton shops of GWR

1857 European and North American Railway, Pointe-du-Chêne to Moncton NB opened.

1859 First Pullman Car

1860 E&NA Railway extended from Moncton to Saint John NB.

1860 Brockville tunnel built, oldest tunnel in Canada.

1864 Appointment of Sandford Fleming to survey for ICR. Report submitted in Feb. 1865. Fleming was placed in charge of ICR surveys in 1863, and served simultaneously as Chief Engineer of the Canadian Pacific (1871), Newfoundland Railway (also 1871).

1867 Section 145 of BNA Act provides for Intercolonial Railway from Halifax to Quebec. (Rivière-du-Loup to Truro to be built)

1867 Brockville & Pembroke Railway completed

1870 Repeal by Parliament of broad-gauge (5ft.6in.) act

1876, 1 July Completion of ICR from Truro to Rivière-du-Loup

1871 Work started on PEI Railway, finished 1873

1872, 16 July Start of surveys for Canadian Pacific Railway.

1875 Start of construction of CPR west of Fort William

1882, 1 January William Van Horne (K.C.M.G.1894) takes over management of CPR

1882 Start of CPR construction west of Winnipeg

1881   Work started on Newfoundland Railway. To Harbour Grace by 1884, completed 1898

1883   Completion Ottawa-Coteau, Canada Atlantic Railway (J.R.Booth)

1885, 7 November   CPR last spike driven at Craigellachie in Eagle Pass

1889, 1 January   Work started on St. Clair River tunnel.

  2 June   CPR "short line" from Montreal to Saint John, NB. opened.

1891, 19 September   Official opening St. Clair tunnel

1896   Mackenzie & Mann acquired charter of Lake Manitoba Railway & Canal Co. that had been granted in 1889. Name changed to Canadian Northern Railway in 1899

1898   Completion of CPR's Montreal Place Viger Station and Hotel

1900, 29 July   Last spike driven on the White Pass and Yukon line

1901   Interprovincial (Alexandra) Bridge between Ottawa and Hull

1903, 30 July   National Transcontinental Railway (NTR) plan announced. Government to build a rail line from Moncton via Quebec to Winnipeg. Incorporation of Grand Trunk Pacific Railway.

1904   CPR Angus Shops opened. Continued in use until the 1990s.

1905, 12 September   First sod of NTR

1906, July   First sod of GTPR

1907, 29 August   Collapse of first Quebec bridge.

1907   CPR builds Empress Hotel in Victoria, BC.

1908, 17 May   electric operation replaces steam through the St. Clair tunnel between Sarnia and Port Huron.

1909, 17 March   Boston to Montreal passenger train crashes into waiting room at Windsor Station, Montreal.

1909   Intercolonial Railway builds new shops in Moncton, NB.

1912, 15 April   Charles Melville Hays, president of the Grand Trunk Railway dies when the *Titanic* sinks. Chateau Laurier hotel, built by the Grand Trunk, opened in Ottawa. Work begins on Mount Royal tunnel for CNoR

1914, 7 April   Grand Trunk Pacific Railway completed. Canadian Government Railways, name gradually replaces ICR.

  4 August   First World War begins.

1915, September   Last spike in CNoR through Rockies

1916   First battalion of Canadian Railway Troops formed.

1916, 11 September   Centre span of redesigned Quebec bridge collapses

1917   CPR officially takes over Allan Line (shipping)

1917, 9 April   Canadians capture Vimy Ridge, greatly aided by the light railway lines built by the Canadian Railway Troops.

1917, September   Completion of redesigned Quebec bridge

CNoR declared bankrupt, taken over by Government

1917, 6 December, 9:06 a.m.   Halifax Explosion. For a list of railway employees killed, see *Canadian Rail* Vol.492 (Jan.-Feb. 2003).

1918, 21 October   Mount Royal Tunnel opened for service.

11 November, 11:00 a.m.   End of First World War

1919, 6 June   Canadian National Railway Company incorporated.

Canadian Government Merchant Marine added to CNR.

1922, 10 October   Sir Henry Thornton made chairman and president of CNR, begins modernization program.

1923, 30 January   Parliament approves amalgamation of Grand Trunk Railway and Canadian National Railway.

5 February   CNR headquarters established in Montreal

1926   CNR equips premier passenger trains with radios to entertain passengers having already established its own radio network.

1927, 6 August   Toronto Union Station, completed in 1921, officially opened by Prince of Wales.

1928   CNR introduces first road diesel engines, Nos. 9000 and 9001.

1929   CPR Royal York Hotel opened in Toronto

October   stock market crash starts Great Depression.

1930   CNR places diesel-electric locomotive 7700 in Service.

1931   Work on Montreal Central Station suspended. CPR Park Avenue Station opened in Montreal.

1932, 12 March   Canadian Railway Historical Association formed.

Punched cards first used by CPR for compiling statistics.

1933   CNR and CPR begin pooling service on passenger train service, between Montreal, Ottawa, Toronto and intermediate points.

1937   CPR acquires first diesel locomotive, No. 7000.

10 April   Trans-Canada Air Lines incorporated, with CNR as sole stockholder.

1939   Royal tour of Canada by King George VI and Queen Elizabeth.

1 September   Germany invades Poland; 3-10 Sept. Second World War begins.

1943, 14 July   CNR Central Station opened in Montreal. Bonaventure Station used for troop trains and commuters, remained in use until 1948. CNR introduces maple leaf insignia.

1945, 7 May   Germany surrenders. 15 Aug. Japan surrenders and Second World War ends.

1950   Diesel Division of General Motors opens London, Ontario, plant. For an overview of diesel development see *Canadian Rail*, No. 464 (May-June 1998).

22 August   Nationwide strike shuts down most Canadian railways. Ended nine days later by Government decree.

1952   Bonaventure Station demolished in Montreal. Dieselization of CPR line through the Rockies.

1955, October   CPR begins diesel service between Montreal and Saint John, NB.

1957   CPR reorganizes, amalgamating many of its wholly owned subsidiaries, so the old companies cease to exist.

1958, 16 April   Queen Elizabeth Hotel opened in Montreal.

1959, June   St. Lawrence Seaway opens.

1960, April–May   end of scheduled steam trains on CN and CP

1961   CNR unveils new logo, still in use today.

CNR moves Montreal headquarters from Grand Trunk offices on McGill St. to office tower adjoining Central Station.

1963, 28 January   CN Archives turned over to Public Archives of Canada

1965, 30 October   Last CN-CP pool train runs between Montreal and Toronto.

1966, 7 January   CPR discontinues transcontinental train the "Dominion."

1971, 17 April   Last rail post-office car, running between Levis and Campbellton makes final trip.

1 May   Amtrak takes over most intercity passenger trains in USA. All trains running into Canada discontinued. Some were reinstated a year or two later.

1977   Via Rail established as subsidiary of CN.

Air Canada becomes separate Crown Corporation

1978, 1 April   Via Rail becomes separate Crown Corporation; purchases all CN & CP passenger equipment

1988, September   Newfoundland railway abandons entire main line and begins tearing up tracks. Some rail service remains in Labrador.

1989, 31 December   All remaining track in Prince Edward Island abandoned.

1992   CPR Angus Shops closed in Montreal. Briefly reopened, then shut down permanently.

1995, 19 November   Shares of CN offered to public.

1996, September   CPR moves headquarters from Montreal to Calgary.

1998, 30 June   VIA Rail abolishes job of Passenger Conductor.

2001, 3 October   CPR splits into five companies: Canadian Pacific Railway, CP Ships, Fairmont Hotels, Fording Coal and Pan Canadian Energy (which has since merged with Alberta Energy to form EnCana Corporation).

Appendix C

Finding Archives,
Museums and Libraries

Internet

On the Internet, the easiest site to find contact information for Archives is the CCA page <www.CdnCouncilArchives.ca/councils.html> [sic the caps]. Click on "Directory of Archives" where you can search by place, name, etc. A place name will produce a list of institutions in that place and a click on any one will produce a screen with full address and contact information. Because many libraries and museums have archives, they will be on the lists.

The University of Saskatchewan offers links to archive Web sites at <www.usask.ca/archives/menu.html>, but you have to use the link, get to the web page and then try to find the "contact us" button. Moreover, the first button you encounter on the first screen will take you directly to Archives Canada. You have to go down about two screens to search by type of archive, or place. "Archives Canada" [formerly CAIN] is where you search for records, it is not all that useful for addresses or contact information.

Library and Archives Canada <www.collectionscanada.ca> will link you to most libraries through their Canadian Library Gateway; there are also lists of special libraries at the site. The Canadian Museum Association in partnership with the Canadian Heritage Information Network has developed an online *Official Directory of Museums and Related Institutions* that you can bring up at <www.museums.ca> if your computer has all the latest bells and whistles. Otherwise, the Canadian Museum of Civilization <www.civilization.ca> offers "Online Resources for Canadian Heritage," click on Museums and Other Cultural Institutions and go to "General and reference works" where you can link to provincial museum associations.

In Print

If you prefer the printed page, you can try asking for the following directories at your nearest reference library, but you must check the addresses given in older editions with a current telephone directory or on the Internet. Most of these country- or continent-wide directories stopped printing books in the 1990s, shifting databases to CD-ROM or the Internet.

Directory of Canadian Archives/Annuaire des services d'archives canadiens. Ottawa: Canadian Council of Archives, 1990. Arranged alphabetical by province. Indexed by name and subjects. Now in the Internet.

Directory of Libraries in Canada. Ed. Lynn Fraser. Toronto: Micromedia Ltd., 7th ed. 1993. Alphabetical, with place, subject and name indexes. Now available on CD-ROM or computer file.

Directory of Associations in Canada. Toronto: Micromedia, revised July 1993. Look for latest edition, available on CD-ROM or Computer file.

Directory of Historical Organizations in the United States and Canada. Ed. & comp. Mary Bray Wheeler. Nashville, TN.: American Association for State and Local History, 14th ed. 1990 /latest ed. 2001. Indexed by place and subject. See 'Transportation' entries.

Guide to Canadian Photographic Archives. Ed. Christopher Seifried. Ottawa: Public Archives of Canada, 1984, very out of date but might be useful.

Official Directory of Canadian Museums and Related Institutions. Ottawa: Canadian Museums Association, last ed. 1997–99. Listed by place, with indexes to personnel, category and name. See sect. 10, Transportation.

[U.S.A. only.] *Official Museum Directory.* Washington, D.C.: American Association of Museums, 23rd ed. 1993.

Railway-related Addresses

Adams, Lawrence. *The Guide to Canada's Railway Heritage Museums and Attractions.* Winnipeg: North Kildonan Publications, 1993. Available from publisher, 28006 - 1453 Henderson Highway, Winnipeg, MB R2G 4E9. The same press issued a revised 2nd edition, compiled by Daryl T. Adair, in 2001, ISBN 0969697105.

Railway Directory and Year Book [year]. Comp. Chris Bushell [1988]. P. Reed Business Publishing Ltd., The Quadrant, Sutton, Surrey SM2 5AS, Great Britain. International, addresses for railways and related companies and associations.

Railway periodicals and association addresses are listed here together since they are often associated. An association, if still active, may have the best collection of its own periodicals. Periodicals marked ** are available on microform; consult the latest catalogue of University Microfilms International.

Trade and Company Periodicals

The Railway and Shipping World, published from March 1898–1905, then as
The Railway & Marine World, from 1906–July 1912, then as
Canadian Railway and Marine World, Aug.1912–Dec.1936, then as
Canadian Transportation, from 1937 - vol.71, No.10, Oct.1968, then
Canadian Transportation & Distribution Management, to Oct.1989,
Canadian Transportation, to Dec. 1990,
Canadian Transportation Logistics, 1991–

** all the above titles available on microform. Also at CRHA Library, and see Canadian Rail, No. 463 (March–April 1998) for Centennial tribute.

Canadian National Railway [now a private company]

Archival holdings, Library and Archives Canada; Dechief Library, holdings dispersed; some at LAC, Ottawa. Photographic Library, some at LAC, the balance is at the Canadian Museum of Science and Technology.

CN Periodicals

Canadian Government Railways Employee Magazine, 1915–Apr.1919
Canadian National Railways Employees Magazine, May 1919–Dec.1921
Canadian National Railways Magazine, 1922–Oct. 1937
Canadian National Magazine, ended 1957,** (1943–1957), replaced by *Keeping Track* **(to Dec. 1974) and Fil du Rail

Canadian Pacific Railway
[a private company, now one of five companies]

Archives: P.O. Box 6042, Station Centreville, Montréal, QC, H3C 3E4

CP Periodicals

Passenger Traffic Bulletin, August 1909–June 1932

Staff Bulletin (newspaper format), June 1934–Dec. 1943
Staff Bulletin (magazine format), Jan. 1944–Sept. 1947, retitled
Spanner (starts with issue #139), Sept. 1947–July 1971
CP Rail News (newspaper), Aug. 1971–1991?
CP Hotel (newspaper), Aug. 1970–June 1977
Dialogue-CP Hotels (newspaper), Jan. 1987–1991?

All CP publications and a computerized index to major articles therein are held at the CP Archives (consult by appointment only). The Index does not include retirements, appointments, transfers or other material of a personal nature.

VIA Rail

Directions, (v.1, no.1, summer 1986–v.3, no.3, spring 1988?)

Other Railroad Periodicals

Alberta Pioneer Railway, *The Marker* [no publication information]
Ontario Northern, *The Quarterly* (1946–1965), The Chevron (1972–).

Union Periodicals

Over the past decade many older railway unions have disappeared as separate entities. In 2004 the Canadian Council of Railway Operating Unions and the Brotherhood of Locomotive Engineers, Canadian Office, became part of

Teamsters Canada Rail Conference
150 Metcalfe St., Suite 1401
Ottawa, ON K2P 1P1
Tel: (613) 235-1828
Fax: (613) 235-1069

Brotherhood of Locomotive Engineers' Journal, published monthly (Cleveland, Ohio: Brotherhood of Locomotive Engineers), began publication in 1867, ended vol.40, no.12 (Dec. 1906). Continued as: *Locomotive engineers journal*, published monthly (Cleveland, Ohio: Brotherhood of Locomotive Engineers), begins with vol.41, no.1 (Jan. 1907), ceased publication with vol.93, no.12 (Dec. 1959).

Trainman News in Canada (Ottawa: Brotherhood of Railway Trainmen), vols. 1–10, no.12 (June 1959–Dec. 1968).

The communiqué - Brotherhood of Railway Running Trades (London, Ont.: Brotherhood of Railway Running Trades), Apr. 1964–.

Brotherhood of Maintenance of Way Employees,
2775 Lancaster Rd., Suite 1
Ottawa, ON K1B 4V8
Tel: (613) 731-7356

Canadian Brotherhood of Railway, Transport and General Workers is now part of the Canadian Auto Workers.

Canadian Railroad employees monthly** (Mar. 1915–1929), then *The Canadian railway employees' monthly*** (Ottawa: Canadian Brotherhood of Railway Employees and Other Transport Workers), from 1930, ended 1953. Continued as: *Canadian transport*** published monthly (irregular) (Ottawa: Canadian Brotherhood of Railway, Transport and General Workers), 1954– .

Canadian Interchange (Ottawa: Brotherhood of Railway, Airline and Steamship Clerks, Freight Handlers, Express and Station Employees; after 1980 Brotherhood of Railway & Airline Clerks), began publication in 1974, ended with no. 57 (June 1987). Continued as: *Interchange Canada* No.58 (Oct. 1987), merged with *Exchange Canada/Echange canadien* (Ottawa: Brotherhood of Railway & Airline Clerks), 1987–.

Topic (London, Ont.: Transportation Employees Canadian Union), vols. 22–28, 1971–

United Transportations Union
71 Bank St.
Ottawa, ON K1P 5N2
Tel: (613) 747-7979

U T U transportation News Canada (Ottawa: United Transportation Union), Jan. 1969–Apr. 1973. *U T U News Canada* (Gloucester, ON: United Transportation Union), May 1973– [monthly to June 1975; bimonthly July/Aug. 1975–1988; quarterly (irregular) 1989–1991.

Locations: Various archives, university and large reference libraries, and Railway Historical Society Collections, may have scattered holdings. The National Library of Canada has an extensive collection, but it is far from complete. Individual unions may prove helpful.

Fan Magazines

Space does not permit an exhaustive list, for such periodicals come and go, change title and so does the emphasis of articles. Two long-established American railway "fan" magazines are currently published and available in Canada. Both have some Canadian content and the advertising covers available railway publications, excursions and many videos.

Railfan & Railroad, Pub: Carstens Publications Inc, P.O. Box 700, Newton, N.J. 07860-0700, USA. tel:(973) 383-3355 fax: (973) 383-4064. Originally *Railroad*, founded 1906. Photo, steam and other railway excursions, and railway-video oriented. <www.carstens-publications. com> and <www.railfan.com>.

Trains, Pub: Kalmbach Publishing Co., 21027 Crossroads Circle, P.O. Box 1612, Waukesha, WI 53187-1612, USA. <www.trainsmag.com> Anecdotes, photographs and railway operations, diesel & steam.

Passenger Train Journal, ceased publication in mid-1996, but back issues are available at several Internet sites. It was published by: Interurban Press, 1741 Gardena Ave., Glendale, CA 91225-0280, USA. tel: (818) 240-9130 and dealt with contemporary intercity rail passenger operations, commuter and transit.

The Railway Magazine, IPC Media Ltd., King's Reach Tower, Stamford Street, London SE1 9LS, England. Published continuously since 1897. Deals with United Kingdom, and some European lines, steam and contemporary equipment oriented. Older issues might be interesting if U.R. started his railway career in the UK.

Railway Associations and Societies

CRHA - Canadian Railroad Historical Association

120, rue St-Pierre
St.-Constant, QC, J5A 2G9
Web site <www.exporail.org>
Publishes *Canadian Rail*, bi-monthly, free to members. Editor: Fred

F. Angus, 3021 Trafalgar Ave., Montreal. P.Q. H3Y 1H3
   e-mail: angus82@aei.ca

Operations and equipment oriented, but with articles on historical subjects as well as current railway news and reviews of many railway-oriented books. There are some published annual indexes and a cumulative index, based on The Ron H. Meyer Memorial Index to C.R.H.A.'s "Canadian Rail" for 1937–1995 (issues #1 to #449) can be consulted on the CRHA Web site.

CRHA Divisions

Web sites of each Division will provide up-to-date information on mailing address, where and when they meet, contacts, etc. Links are found on the CRHA Web site under Divisions. Many have affiliations with local railway museums.

New Brunswick Division
Salem & Hillsborough Railroad
2847 Main Street,
Hillsborough, NB E4H 2X7

Vallée-Jonction Division
397 boulevard Rousseau
Vallée-Jonction, QC G0S 3J0

St. Lawrence Valley Division
P.O. Box 22, Station 'B'
Montreal, QC. H3B 3J5

Rideau Valley Division
P.O. Box 962
90 William St.
Smiths Falls, ON K7A 5A5
Operate Smiths Falls Railway Museum, May through Oct.

Kingston Division
P.O. Box 1714
Kingston, ON K7A 5V5

Toronto & York Division
99 Atlantic Ave., Unit 58
Toronto, ON M6K 3J8

T&Y Division Archives (open by appointment)
527B Mount Pleasant Rd., Toronto ON M4S 2M48
Tel: 416-536-2894 (messages are retrieved weekly)
Publishes *The Turnout* 9 issues p/a: (Sep.1972–)

Niagara Division
P.O.Box 20311
Grantham Postal Outlet
St-Catharines, ON L2M 7W7

Calgary & S. Western Division
Calgary AB
See Web site for current mailing address

Selkirk Division
P.O. Box 2561
Revelstoke, BC V0E 2S0

Pacific Coast Division
P.O. Box 1006, Station 'A'
Vancouver, BC V6C 2P1
Issues *Sandhouse Newsletter*, quarterly, (Apr.1976–)

Prince George-Nechako-Fraser Division
P.O. Box 2408
Prince George, BC V2N 2S6

Esquimalt and Nanaimo Division
2414 Dryfe St.
Victoria, BC V8R 5T2

Other Railway Interest Groups

Bytown Railway Society Inc. (1969)
P.O. Box 141, Station "A"
Ottawa, ON K1N 8V1

Tel: 613-745-1201 [message machine]
Publishes *Branchline: Canada's Rail Newsmagazine*, bi-monthly.

Locomotive and Railway Historical Society of Western Canada,
2120 Southland Dr. S.W., Suite #4104
Calgary, AB T2A 4W3
Fax: 403-261-1057

Midwest Rail Association, Inc.
167 Lombard Ave., #1024
Winnipeg, MB R3B 0T4
Tel:204-942-4632
Publishes *Milepost*, Mandate: To conserve archives and document Railway heritage of Western Canada.

Scotian Railway Society [records and collection at PANS]
Published *The Maritime Express*, (June 1968–Winter 1976).

Upper Canada Railway Society
Box 122, Station "A"
Toronto, ON M5W 1A2
Published *Rail and Transit* (Nov/Dec 1975–Nov/Dec 1979) Newsletter *Informer* (1980–)

West Coast Railway Association (WCRA)
P.O. Box 2790
Vancouver, BC V6B 3X2
Publishes *WCRA News*, monthly.

Railway-related Associations and Institutes

Association of American Railroads
50 F St. N.W.
Washington, D.C. 20001-1564 U.S.A.
Tel: 202-639-2100
Fax: 202-639-5546
www.aar.org/

Canada Institute for Scientific and Technical Information,
National Research Council
1500 Montreal Road
Ottawa, ON K1A 0R6
Tel: 1-800-668-1222
Fax: 613-925-9112.
Main library has a specialized railway collection and may be a source
for interlibrary loans.

Canadian Institute of Guided Ground Transport
(formerly associated with Queens University, Kingston, Ontario)

Canadian Railway Club [formed, 1903; incorporated 1913]
P.O. Box 162, Station "A"
Montreal, Que., H3C 1C5
Web site: www.c-r-c.ca
Published *Canadian Railway Club* News (v.1–, Jan. 1979–)

Canadian Museums Association, Technology and Transport Group
208 Metcalfe, Suite 400
Ottawa, ON K2P 1P7
Tel: 613-567-0099
Web site: www.museums.ca

National Postal Museum is now with the Canadian Museum of
Civilization in Gatineau, QC.
Tel: 613-76-8200

National Museum of Science and Technology
1867 St. Laurent Blvd., P.O. Box 9724
Ottawa, ON K1G 5A3
tel: 613-91-3044
fax: 613-990-3654
Offers the railway buff the opportunity to climb all over wonderful
old engines and cars.

Glossary

"Like the steam locomotive that spawned it, the sprightly and salty vocabulary of the high <line> may belong to an era of railroading that has ended." (PANS, MG1, vol.2470 "Hunter Papers")

So wrote George Alexander Hunter, a Conductor with the CNR, and a member of the Brotherhood of Railway Trainmen for over 65 years. In a small notebook he set down some terms he knew.

An official who disciplines an employee is a Brass Hat.

To train crews trying to make schedules a dispatcher is a train detainer.

A yard master is a ring master, big shot, scissor bill, or King; his office from which the orders come knoledge [sic] box or G.H.Q.

A Yard office clerk is a number dummy.

Outside [yard] checkers are called mud hops.

A Caboose is a waycar but hardly any railroader calls it that it is usually Crummy, dog house, hearse, ape waggon, cage, pallace[sic], shanty, bed house, library, chariot, baceneer[sic] or hack.

Tank town is a small village where there [is] a water tank.

Jerkwater is another term applied to a small town after the railroads adopted the track pan or trough where the water was forced into the tender or tank of the engine by dropping a scoop in the trough as the train was proceeding forcing the water into the tank—taking water on the fly as it was sometimes known.

An engineer is a hogger to almost everyone but himself or another engineer.

A Conductor is a Captain or the Brains to his crew but never to himself he is never anything but a Conductor when he talks of his job.

— ♦ —

The following glossary is less "salty" but may explain various jobs and aspects of railroading in the era of steam:

Air Brakes   The key to modern safe railroading. Introduced in passenger service about 1880 and in freight service after 1893 when the U.S. Congress passed the Safety Appliance Act.

Boomer   Itinerant railwaymen who moved from job to job, "pulling the pin" (quitting railroad job) at short notice for various reasons.

Brakeman   Originally, what the name implies, he who set the mechanical brakes on the individual cars (passenger or freight) when whistled for by the engineer. Not a pleasant employment on top of a freight train in a Canadian winter. A freight train would have a head-end brakemen and a rear-end brakeman; a passenger train, one or two brakemen depending on its length. With the arrival of air-brakes the official term became "Trainman," but the original name hung on.

Bridge & Building Master   Responsible for bridges and buildings (as opposed to roadbed and track).

"Bumping"   Process of using accumulated seniority to "bid in" a desirable job occupied by someone else. "Bumpee" was then entitled to bump someone else lower down the seniority list.

Call-Board   Notice-board where call notices for crews were posted.

Call-Boy   Boy employed (in pre-telephone era) to find and roust out crews required for "extra" and unscheduled trains.

Car-knocker   Car maintenance man. Known to passengers as the men who walked the length of each passenger train at designated points, tapping each wheel with a hammer. A wheel that has a defect will make a slightly different sound from a normal one.

Carman   Car maintenance man, passenger and freight.

Chief Clerk   Senior administrative officer, reports to a Superintendent (of whatever function).

Conductor   Person in charge of a train, passenger or freight. He was in charge, like the captain of the ship. The engineer (engine driver) was second-in-command, but was outranked by the conductor.

Dispatcher (or Despatcher)   Official responsible for scheduling and supervising train movements from a central point (usually division point).Trains listed on published operating timetable can operate in accordance with this published timetable, but *any and all* changes from this and any "special" or "extra" trains or other changes must be authorized by the Dispatcher.

Division   Geographical portion of a railway line. See Chapter One.

Division Engineer   Engineer responsible for roadbed, track, bridges and buildings for a specific division.

Extra   An unlisted, unscheduled train, operated as the need or demand arose. Designated by the locomotive number and carrying white flags and white marker lights.

Engineer   North American terminology for locomotive [engine]-driver. Slang term "hog" or "hogger."

Fireman   North American term for stoker. Job consisted of shovelling several tons of coal each run and watching for and confirming signals with engineer if no head-end brakeman.

Hostler   Mechanic/caretaker responsible for care, feeding and short movements of locomotives in yards not hauling trains.

Hotbox (overheated bearing)   If not found and dealt with can lead to derailment and serious accident. Routinely watched for by crews of meeting or passing trains and station and yard personnel.

Locomotive Foreman   Assigns locomotives to trains and runs.

Master car builder   Responsible for maintenance and condition of all railway cars, freight and passenger.

Master mechanic   Responsible for maintenance and condition of motive power (locomotives).

Operator   Telegraph operator, see Station Agent.

Order Board   Signals at a station or office indicating whether a train may proceed beyond that station or not. Usually a red light with a horizontal arm (stop), green light with vertical arm (clear or go ahead).

Passing Track   Sidetrack to allow trains to meet on single track line, or overtake on single or double track line.

Profile   A drawing showing track gradients along a length of a railway line. Often found in lists of Railway records, a "profile" is neither a portrait nor a biographical sketch.

Roadmaster   Responsible for roadbed and track maintenance. Section foremen and crews report to him.

Section   Portion of track within a Division, maintained by Section crew.

Section [of a train]   If a train was too long, for whatever reason, it might run in several "sections" which were so identified. Only the passage of the last section constituted the passage of the "train" past a point.

Spare List   People in running trades who did not have sufficient seniority to be assigned regular runs were on the "spare list," whence they were called up when and as required. Also, a brakeman or fireman who was qualified as a conductor or engineer but didn't have enough seniority could be on the "spare list" for conductor or engineer.

Station Agent   Person responsible for all business, usually including train movements, at small to medium sized stations. Might have one or more assistants or "operators" (telegraph operators).

Tower   Catchall term for wayside signal tower. May control signals, switches and interlockers, lift bridge and other functions.

Train Line   On a passenger train, a pneumatic signalling system from the cars to the locomotive. Engineer responded with whistle signals from the locomotive.

Train Orders   Written instructions governing train movements issued by the Dispatcher.

Wye   A triangle with a tail, a track arrangement whereby locomotives or trains can reverse direction. Although they can operate in reverse, most steam locomotives were designed to run primarily in one direction. All freight cars and most passenger cars can operate in either direction, although it is usual for passenger train equipment to be turned around at the end of the run, so that baggage cars are next to the locomotive and other cars in their accustomed places. Backing up a full train is not easy. By backing down one arm of the wye into the tail and coming out the other arm the train can reverse direction in relative safety.

Yardmaster   Responsible for directing train movements within designated "yard limits."

A fuller, and saltier, "Lingo of the Rails" is found in Freeman Hubbard's *Encylopedia of North American Railroading*, pp. 185–197, Appendix B.

Bibliography and Works Consulted

Bibliographies of Canadian Railways

Dechief, Hélène. *A Bibliography of Published Material and Theses on Canadian Railways.* Montreal: CN Library, 1980. Divided by subject: sections on CN . CP, regional lines, biographies, union histories, rolling stock, hotels, etc.

Lewis, Grace S. *Bibliographical List of References to Canadian Railways 1829–1938.* Ottawa: Dept. of Trade & Commerce, Dominion Bureau of Statistics Library, 1938. Articles, reports and books arranged by year of publication, alphabetical within year. Index to subjects and authors, chronological arrangement makes it hard to use.

Tennant, R.D. Jr. *The Quill and Rail Catalogue.* Halifax, Nova Scotia: The Tennant Publishing House, 1976. Bibliography of older publications (pre 1976, divided into Government and non-government publications.

Railroading in British Columbia. Comp. Ron Meyer. Vancouver: Pacific Coast Division, C.R.H.A., 1993. Expanded and updated from the 1973 edition. 114 pp. "For anyone looking for data on the railways of British Columbia, or even on Canadian Railways in general, this work is a real gold-mine of information on where articles can be found." F.F.Angus, *Canadian Rail* No.434, May-June 1993.

Who's Who and Biography

Biographical Directory of the Railway Officials of America. Chicago: Railway Age Pub. Co., 1885–1930. After 1930 published as: *Who's Who in Railroading in North America.* New York: Simmons-Boardman, ca. 1930–1968. Then as *Who's Who in Railroading and Rail Transit.* New York: Simmons-Boardman, 1971–1985 -? A valuable serial. Title and imprint varies from edition to edition.

Locations: The best collection is at York University, Toronto [OTY] with 1887, 1896, 1901, 1906, 1922, 1946, 1954, 1971, 1983, 1985 and probably more. Large reference libraries usually have one or two editions, and this is the sort of book that turns up in railway museums and historical society collections.

Works Consulted

Andreae, Christopher and Geoffrey Matthews. *Lines of Country: An Atlas of Railway and Waterway History in Canada*, Erin ON: The Boston Mills Press, 1997. Definitive data on railways and canals.

Angus, Fred F. "The Centennial of the Railway and Marine World," *Canadian Rail*, No. 463 (March–April 1998), pp. 47–56.

Barr, Eleanor. "And the C.P.R. Said Let There Be Division Points …," *Canadian Rail*, No. 380 (May–June 1984), pp. 76–81.

Bennett, Carol & D.W. McCuaig. *In Search of the K & P*. Renfrew, Ont.: Renfrew Advance, 1982. Arranged by Station with considerable information on individuals. Bibliography, no index.

Berton, Pierre. *The National Dream: The Great Railway 1871–1881* and *The Last Spike: The Great Railway 1881–1885*. Toronto, Montreal: McClelland & Stewart Ltd., 2 vols., 1970 and 1971. Each volume is indexed, with bibliographies as well as a detailed "Chronology" of the years covered. Some maps, no illustrations.

Booth, J. Derek. *Railways of Southern Quebec* (2 vols.), Toronto: Railfare Enterprises Ltd., 1982, 1985. Both volumes are indexed, annotated, with excellent bibliographies, maps and many illustrations.

Butlin, Noel G. *Finding List of Canadian Railway Companies Before 1916*. Washington and Boston, A.R.A. 1953. Chronological list only.

Calliste, Agnes. "Sleeping Car Porters in Canada; An Ethnically Submerged Labour Market," *Canadian Ethnic Studies/Etudes Ethniques au Canada*, Vol. XIX, No. 1, 1987.

Clark, W.W. *Clark's History of the Early Railways in Nova Scotia*. [1925]. Not indexed, anecdotal, actually concerns the Dominion Atlantic Railway and its earlier components.

Coo, Bill. *Scenic Rail Guide to Central and Atlantic Canada; Scenic Rail Guide to Western Canada*. Various editions and revised editions, through the 1980s. Traces the VIA Rail routes across Canada. Contains detailed information on geographic features and much railway history and lore about places along the lines.

Craven, Paul and Tom Traves. "Canadian Raiways as Manufacturers, 1850–1880." *Historical Papers*. Canadian Historical Association, 1883.

Currie, A.W. *The Grand Trunk Railway of Canada*. Toronto: U. of Toronto Press, 1957. Fully indexed, extensive notes but no bibliography. Includes map of "Railways Forming the Grand Trunk System in Ontario & Quebec with Their Original Names." Concerns business rivalry with CPR, so includes information on both systems.

Dorman, Robert. *A Statutory History of the Steam & Electric Railways of Canada 1836–1937*. Appendix [maps]. Ottawa: King's Printer, 1937.

Dorman, Robert and D.E. Stoltz. [revised edition] *A Statutory History of Railways of Canada 1836-1986*. Kingston, Ont.: Queens Univ., Canadian Institute of Guided Ground Transport, 1987. This revised edition is the definitive listing of railway companies and their various corporate incarnations.

The Encyclopedia of Canada. General ed. W. Stewart Wallace. Toronto: University Associates of Canada, 6 vols. (1935–37; registered ed. 1940; 2nd ed. 1948). Gives brief histories of many companies under the name of the line; in addition, most town and city entries say which railway lines served the community.

Filby, James. *Credit Valley Railway, 'The Third Giant': a history*. Cheltenham, Ont.: The Boston Mills Press, 1974. Bibliography, no index.

Gibbon, John M. *Steel of Empire: the Romantic History of the Canadian Pacific*. Toronto: McClelland & Stewart, 1935. Index, brief bibliography. Politics and VIPs.

Gillham, Lionel F. *Just a Few Lines: the Story of Canada's First Railway, The Champlain & St. Lawrence Rail Road*. Rotherham, S. Yorkshire, England: the author, ca.1994.

Glazebrook, G.P. de T. *A History of Transportation in Canada*. Toronto: Ryerson Press, 2 Vols., 1938; reprinted Toronto: McClelland & Stewart Ltd., 1964 (The Carleton Library, Nos. 11 and 12). Annotated and indexed, no bibliography.

Graham, Allan. *A Photo History of the Prince Edward Island Railway*. Printed by William & Crue Ltd., 2000.

Hubbard, Freeman. *Encyclopedia of North American Railroading*. New York, Toronto: McGraw Hill Books, 1976. A fascinating survey of railroad history and lore, many entries concern Canadian Railways.

Lamb, W. Kaye. *History of the Canadian Pacific Railway*. New York: Macmillan, 1977. (Vol.5 in Railroads of America Series). Fully indexed, with excellent bibliography.

Legget, Robert F. *Railroads of Canada*. Vancouver: Douglas, David & Charles, 1973 (Railroad Histories of the World Series). Well indexed, with many (but not all) lines listed under Railways; suggested reading list. Text includes a concise history of most railway lines, from 1836 to 1971.

Linley, Bill. *Canadian Pacific in Colour*, Volume 1, Eastern Lines, 2003.

List of Canadian Patents…Ottawa: MacLean, Roger & Co., 1882; facsimile edition, Ottawa: Gordon Publications and Reproductions, 1979.

Lovering, Cynthia. *General Guide Series: Government Archives Division*. Ottawa: National Archives of Canada, 1991.

MacKay, Donald. *The Asian Dream: The Pacific Rim and Canada's National Railway*. Vancouver, Toronto: Douglas & McIntyre, 1986.

MacKay, Donald. *The People's Railway: A History of the Canadian National*. Vancouver: Douglas & McIntyre, 1992. This more current history carries forward the story of the Canadian National into the 1980s. Bibliography, index, chronology, maps and photographs. First two chapters provide a clear, concise account of how and when the various components of CN came together.

MacKay, Donald and Lorne Perry. *Train Country: An Illustrated History of CN*. Vancouver: Douglas & McIntyre, 1994. 150 photos, plus reminiscences of people who worked for the railway.

Mann, Thomas. *The Oxford Guide to Library Research*. Oxford, New York: Oxford University Press, 1998.

McDougall, J. Lorne. *Canadian Pacific*. Montreal: McGill U. Press, 1968). Written for the CPR. Contains a List of Railways mentioned in the text (pp.167–179). Not all are CPR, nor are all CPR lines listed.

McKee, Bill and Georgeen Klassen. *Trail of Iron: The CPR and the Birth of the West, 1880–1930*. Vancouver, Toronto: Glenbow-Alberta Institute, 1983. Picture book, with index and CPR-related bibliography.

McNeil, Bill and Morris Wolfe. *The Birth of Radio in Canada: Signing On*. Toronto: Doubleday Canada Ltd. 1982.

Nason, Dave. *Railways of New Brunswick*. Fredericton N.B.: New Ireland Press, 1992. Covers planning and building of all lines in New Brunswick, maps, pictures, notes and bibliography.

Nock, O.S. *Algoma Central Railway*. London: A. & C. Black. 1975. Indexed, well illustrated.

Official Railway Guide or *Canadian Official Railway Guide* or *International Railway and Steam Navigation Guide*... [title varies; published since 1864]. The publisher's archive is owned by the University of Guelph library, which updated and published the final edition in 1991. Collection is described by G.T. Bloomfield in *The Shipper's Bible: An Introduction to the Canadian Guide Collection* (Guelph, Ont., 1993). The collection is virtually complete from 1893 to 1991. Early issues (to 1915) are available in microform (Canadiana Microforms, 1987).

Ontario Historical Society Papers and Records

Breithaupt, Wm. H. 'The Railways of Ontario', vol. 25, 1929.

Ferris, Terry. "Railways of British North America," vol.38, 1946.

Smith, R.D. "The Northern Railway: Its Origins and Construction, 1834–1855," vol.48, 1956. Check cumulative index for other papers.

O'Reilly, Susan McLeod. *On Track: The Railway Mail Service In Canada*. Hull, QC: Canadian Museum of Civilization, 1992. Annotated and illustrated, list of 'Oral Sources', no index.

Québec, Government of. *Le Réseau Ferroviaire Québec. 1986*. In French, but with easy to follow tables and charts, this concise report on Quebec's provincial railway network includes tables listing sub-divisions (their terminal stations and mileage) for CN, CP, as well as small regional and industrial lines.

Richards, Tom. *Was Your Grandfather a Railwayman?* Birmingham, UK: F.F.H.S., 2nd ed. 1989, now in its 4th ed.

Sanford, Barrie. *McCulloch's Wonder—The Story of the Kettle Valley Railway.* Vancouver: 1977. Brief index and bibliography.

Sarsfield, Mairuth. *No Crystal Stair: a novel.* Norval ON: Moulin Pub., c 1997; Toronto: Stoddard, 1998.

Sessional Papers of the Dominion of Canada [SP]. Ottawa: Queen's/King's Printer, 1868–1923. Continued in part as *Annual Departmental Reports.*

Smith, Douglas N.W. *Canadian Rail Passenger Yearbook,* then *Canadian Rail Passenger Review.* Ottawa; Trackside Canada, 1993 - , an annual publication with articles and photographs on railways, both contemporary and historic.

Stephens, David E. *Iron Roads: Railways of Nova Scotia.* Windsor, N.S.: Lancelot Press, 1972.

Stevens, G.R. *Canadian National Railways.* Toronto, Vancouver: Clarke Irwin, 2 vols., 1960, 1962). Each vol. fully indexed. Vol. I 1836–1896 (largely Grand Trunk and ICR) Vol. 2 1896-1922 (everything else).

Towards CN: from portage railway to a national system. Catalogue to an exhibition prepared by the Public Archives of Canada … , comp. Carl Vincent & Lloyd Chisamore. Ottawa, Public Archives of Canada, 1972.

Trout, J.M. and Edwd. *The Railways of Canada for 1870-71 shewing the Progress … and Organization of the Railways of the Dominion …* Toronto: 1871 and facsimile, Coles Publishing, 1970. Alphabetical list of railways built or proposed in 1871. Material may not be accurate.

Tucker, Albert. *Steam Into Wilderness: Ontario Northland Railway 1902–1962.* Toronto: Fitzhenry & Whiteside, 1978. Index, maps, chronology, many interviews with individuals.

Turner, Robert D. *Railroaders.* Victoria, B.C.: Sound and Moving Image Div., Provincial Archives of B.C., 1981 (Sound Heritage Series, No. 31). Interviews with workers on various railways in British Columbia; filled with personal accounts and railway lore. Chronology for British Columbia

Vincent. Carl. *RG 46 Records of the Canadian Transport Commission, Federal Archives Division, General Inventory Series.* Ottawa: PAC, 1984.

Wickberg, Edgar, ed. *From China to Canada: a history of the Chinese communities in Canada.* Toronto: McClelland & Stewart in association with the Multicultural Directorate, Dept. of the Secretary of State, c. 1982.

Woods, Shirley E. *Cinders and Saltwater: the Story of Atlantic Canada's Railways.* Halifax, N.S.: Nimbus Pub., 1992. Covers all four Atlantic provinces from the beginnings to the present; with emphasis on building railroads. Indexed, illustrated, extensive bibliography.

Wright, Glenn. *RG 43 Records of the Department of Railways and Canals, Federal Archives Division, General Inventory Series.* Ottawa: PAC, 1986.

Index

Other fine books by Althea Douglas

Help I've Inherited an Attic Full of History second revised edition "What do I do with all this stuff?" is the plea of those who find themselves the custodians of a portion of history. Included are simple conservation procedures, and extensive "not-before" lists to help date the objects.
2003 184p 0-7779-2129-4 **$33.00**

The Family Treasures Book
The 40th Anniversary Keepsake Project
Use this handy treasure book to keep track of your treasures
2001 40p 0-7779-2123-5 **$2.00/free** with the purchase of *Help! I've Inherited an Attic Full of History*

Here be Dragons! Navigating the Hazards Found in Canadian Family Research
Researchers are aided with advice on changing social customs, common knowledge that is now forgotten, migration patterns and the splits and mergers that formed today's religious denominations.
1996 74p 0-7779-0196-X **$14.00**

Here be Dragons, Too! More Navigational Hazards for the Canadian Family Researcher
Moves beyond standard genealogical sources to examine other records. Includes advice on privacy and on computer research.
2000 88p 0-7779-0224-9 **$14.00**

Tools of the Trade for Canadian Genealogy 2nd edition
Althea Douglas
Praise for the first edition: "Such wide-ranging knowledge dispensed by an expert, especially with references to the work of local genealogy and history societies, reinforces... that ...not everything can be found on the Internet. Douglas has produced another gem ... to ease the complexities and diversities of seeking Canadian ancestors." – Brenda Dougall Merriman, CGRS, CGL, *National Genealogical Society Quarterly*, 2000
Updated, revised and indexed. The extensive resource list includes Web addresses and other contact information.
2003 136p resources index 0-7779-2134-0 **$21.95**

More Tools of the Trade from the OGS

About Genealogical Standards of Evidence second edition
Brenda Dougall Merriman
How to properly document your research.
2004 0-7779-2135-9 **$16.00**

Genealogy in Ontario: Researching the Records revised third edition
Brenda Dougall Merriman
A must-have book for anyone with Ontario roots!
2002 278p 0-7779-2127-8 **$37.00**

The Genealogist's Journal
Susan Smart
Handy record book with hints to help your research and space for your valuable notes.
2003 112 p wiro binding hard card backing 0-7779-2130-8 **$14.95**